The French Armies in the
Seven Years' War

Lee Kennett

The French Armies in the Seven Years' War

A study in military organization and administration

Duke University Press
Durham, N. C. 1967

Library of Congress Catalogue card number 67–18529. Printed in the United States of America by Kingsport Press, Inc., Kingsport, Tennessee.

Preface

Eighteenth-century Europe resounded with the noise of war. One authority has calculated that in only two of the hundred years after 1700 was the continent completely at peace. The century opened with the victories of Marlborough; its middle years saw the flowering of Frederick the Great's genius; it closed as Napoleon's star was rising. Quite logically the age has attracted the interest of generations of military historians. Students of the period who wish to follow the clash of armies at Blenheim or Rosbach may choose from scores of studies. Indeed, the mass of historical material on eighteenth-century wars is so vast that no author can add to the mountain of literature without a word of justification to his readers.

As its title implies, the present work is not a military history in the conventional sense. The author has chosen the French Army in the period of the Seven Years' War as a means of illustrating certain aspects and problems of warfare two centuries ago that have seldom been treated by historians. The book constitutes a sort of marginalia to the conflicts of the eighteenth century, and if it is useful in this way its modest purpose will have been achieved.

Many people and institutions gave freely of advice and assistance. The author owes a special debt of gratitude to Professor Oron J. Hale of the University of Virginia, who supervised the manuscript's long and labored genesis as a doctoral dissertation. Professors Theodore Ropp and Harold Parker of Duke University gave liberally of their time and knowledge, as did Professor George Taylor of the University of North Carolina and Professor André Corvisier of the University of Nantes. The United States Government made possible a year's research in Paris through a grant under the Fulbright Act. The authorities of the Service historique de l'Armée and the Bibliothèque municipale de Nancy generously placed at the author's disposal the wealth of manuscript material from which the work is chiefly drawn.

Contents

Introduction

The Seven Years' War was a decisive event in the history of France of the *ancien régime*. The nation entered the conflict without enthusiasm, fought without distinction, and emerged from it without victory. The long struggle perceptibly weakened the ties which had bound the people of France to the dynasty for a thousand years, and in its course it took the country far down the road which led to the cataclysm of 1789. The strain of war revealed as never before the serious shortcomings of the royal government; to compound the damage, the military defeats, the financial crises, and the political instability occurred precisely at a time of great intellectual ferment. The first volume of Diderot's *Encyclopédie* appeared on the eve of the war, in 1751—the date which the French historian Mornet assigns for the beginning of the second and critical phase in the intellectual origins of the French Revolution.

Had France won the war, the regime might have bolstered its sagging prestige and perhaps averted, or at least postponed, the events of 1789. Had she even lost it in a more spectacular way, the shock of defeat might have jolted the royal government from its fatal complacency and *immobilisme* and brought it onto some other less disastrous course. The war was never popular in France, perhaps more than anything else because French public opinion—such as it existed in the period—never felt that the vital interests of the nation were involved. Prussia fought for the most pressing of all motives: survival. Austria, or at least her sovereign, fought for revenge and for Silesia. The English fought, as only they could, for the colonial and maritime stakes so vital to them.

French war aims were not so clear. Extension of the north-eastern frontiers, traditionally a goal of French monarchs, was in this case impossible. The ill-starred and unpopular alliance with the Hapsburgs obliged Louis XV to respect the territorial integrity of the Austrian Netherlands. The prospect of colonial acquisitions did not rouse the same enthusiasm as among the *mercanti* across the channel. Though an empire was lost in 1763, the peace seemed more humiliating than costly. Every student of the eighteenth century remembers how Voltaire dismissed the cession of Canada to England as the loss of "a few acres of snow." Apathy and hostility toward the war itself were marked: the courtiers mocked; the philosophers redoubled their assaults on the existing order; the vast mass of Frenchmen knew the war only through unpleasant contacts with the tax collector and the recruiting officer.

In military circles the defeats of the years 1756–1763 produced a feeling of frustration and a searching self-criticism. Already an occasional officer, sensing in the mood of the nation an echo of his own troubled mind, thought he could see in the *débâcle*—more clearly than he realized—"the signal for the approaching destruction of our monarchy." [1] From the war also proceeded a desire for reform, though this was much less well defined. War in the mid-eighteenth century was in process of rapid transition. Armies were becoming more mobile—or striving to become so. Winter campaigns were becoming more common, and the leisurely siege warfare of the previous era less so. Important innovations were being made in tactics and armament. The response to, and in many cases the reaction against, all these changes was to stir French military thought for the next quarter century.

The history of the Seven Years' War has been written

1. Marquis de Caraman, "Réflexions sur l'état présent du militaire en France." This manuscript of 1758 is as found in André Dussauge, *Etudes sur la Guerre de Sept Ans. Le ministère de Belle-Isle: Krefeld et Lütterberg (1758)* (Paris, 1914), p. 273.

many times.[2] The purpose of this work is not to recount what the French Army did or failed to do, but rather to examine that army as an institution. Occasionally Frenchmen of the period referred to their military establishment as a "machine." To examine the nature and the workings of this machine, along with its various parts, and the ways in which they functioned or failed to function, is the object of the present inquiry.

The logical beginning for the study proposed here is the *primum mobile* of the machine, the royal government. Through the agency of command the motive force is transmitted to the members, the field armies. The composition and organization of these units will be examined in their turn, along with the various staff and logistical functions which permitted their maintenance and operation. French historical work on the period of the Seven Years' War is particularly deficient in this regard. Relatively few historians have been attracted to a period so bleak in French military annals. Matters of military administration appear only as brief digressions in the works of Pajol and Waddington, the "classical" military historians of the late nineteenth century. This dearth of information has occasionally been remedied by obscure and technical monographs by French officers, studies which in most cases appeared before 1914. The sum of all this work leaves some questions only partially answered and others completely untouched. For this reason archival sources, letters, journals, and other materials of the period have been of

2. The standard French accounts are Richard Waddington, *La Guerre de Sept Ans* (5 vols., Paris, 1894–1907), and General Charles-Pierre-Victor Pajol, *Les guerres sous Louis XV* (7 vols., Paris, 1881–1891). The official Prussian account is *Der Siebenjährige Krieg* (13 vols., Berlin, 1901–1914), the work of the Historical Section of the German General Staff. Austrian participation in the conflict is covered in Alfons Freiherr von Wrede and Anton Senek, *Geschichte der Kaiserlichen und Königlichen Wehrmacht. Die Regimenten, Korps, Branchen und Anstalten von 1618 bis Ende des 19 Jahrhunderts* (5 vols., Vienna, 1898–1905). The standard British account is in the second volume of J. W. Fortescue, *A History of the British Army* (London, 1910).

primary importance. Occasionally even the primary sources have failed to provide more than a conjectural answer.[3]

What is the value and the justification of the study proposed here? First of all, it may contribute to a clearer understanding of the army itself, an institution of fundamental importance in the history of France. Further, it may provide a partial explanation for the mediocre success of French armies from 1756 to 1763. Here the study must become comparative. By examining the Armée du Roi side by side with the armed forces of George II, Frederick the Great, and Maria Theresa it is possible to draw some worthwhile conclusions concerning the success of Louis XV's government in that most serious business for any government, the prosecution of war. Moreover, such an inquiry can provide a view of eighteenth-century France in reduced scale where the proportions are more manageable. The army reflected faithfully the government and the society it defended. It was the old regime in microcosm, with all its characteristics and weaknesses. It was a fortress of privilege and inequality, which withstood the assaults of the *roturier* to the last. Wedded to a glorious past that stretched back to Bouvines and Marignano, it was loath to part with an enormous and cumbersome baggage of tradition. Its deep conservatism successfully resisted thoroughgoing reform; Turgot had his military counterparts in Choiseul and Saint Germain, who could only administer palliatives to a patient who refused to be cured.

Lastly, the author has tried to bring into view certain aspects of eighteenth-century warfare that have been somewhat neglected. War is, after all, the most taxing social activity man has yet devised for himself; its every facet has its importance. Victory and defeat depend only partly on the skill of generals

3. This is particularly true of the matter of military finances. The defective accounting practices then existing gave Louis XV and his ministers only an approximate idea of their fiscal resources, and the picture is even more obscured for modern historians by the destruction of many documents during the Commune uprising.

and the vagaries of the goddess of battles. Every army standing in battle array—whether good, bad, or indifferent—is the culmination of a vast effort in marshaling human and material resources. These mundane considerations of men, money, and matériel tend to pale before the high drama of a pitched battle; perhaps this accounts for the lack of emphasis. In any event, these factors are seldom given their due.

Much of this book is devoted to what might be called the French "war effort," though it may seem strange to apply this modern term to the warfare of two centuries ago. Traditionally the era was one of limited war which made only moderate demands upon the population and sought a limited goal which fell far short of "total victory" and the annihilation of the enemy. By modern standards the war effort was unimpressive at best. Governments had yet to tap to the fullest the springs of nationalism. Rulers lacked the modern techniques for gauging the resources of their countries and channeling them toward a military end. Even Louis XIV, that most absolute of monarchs, would have envied the thoroughness and efficiency with which a local draft board of today siphons up manpower. Yet each of the European powers in the mid-eighteenth century was making conscious and earnest efforts to realize more efficiently its war potential. In a sense the transition to total war had begun.

An apology to the reader is perhaps in order for saying so little in the present study about the colonial and maritime theaters of the war which loom so large in American and English history. The reasons for this omission—admittedly a large one—are twofold: first, these aspects of the war are fraught with special difficulties. The colonial war particularly presented the eighteenth-century military establishments with full as many problems as guerilla warfare presents to the sophisticated war machines of today. The rules were different; classical tactics were often not suitable to the terrain; the use of native populations in the war, numerous but untrained, dictated further modifications; questions of logistics were far more complicated.[4] Essentially a land power, France fought here at great disadvantage. Once the conflict began, the resources she could commit were limited;[5] the logistical problems were insuperable. Second, the French themselves saw the war as one to be won or lost on the Continent. They relied heavily on native manpower in the colonies and on the militia for coastal defense. Almost the totality of the regular army was committed in Germany. There the maximum effort was made and there the government sought victories and conquests to offset colonial reverses. It is there, pitted in conventional warfare, that the French military establishment can best be seen and judged.

Since the campaigns and battles are referred to only incidentally in the course of this work, it would be well at this point to give a very brief synopsis of the military operations. The French armies were chiefly opposed by an allied army comprised of contingents from Hanover, Hesse, Brunswick-Lüneburg, and England. This allied army was first commanded by the Duke of Cumberland, but after the abortive capitulation of Closter-Zeven, Cumberland was replaced by the able Duke Ferdinand of Brunswick-Lüneburg. For six years the armies moved back and forth through Germany with most of the campaigning confined to the rough rectangle formed by the Weser, Main, and Rhine rivers and the sea.

In 1756 the French government was not ready to send an army into Germany, and the chief military effort in Europe was directed at Minorca, conquered by the Duke of Richelieu

4. The very special nature of warfare in the New World has been admirably described in the recent work of Howard H. Peckham, *The Colonial Wars, 1689–1762* (Chicago, 1964).

5. In 1758 the total forces of the kingdom numbered 395 battalions and 236 squadrons; there were twelve battalions in Canada and four in India. "Emplacement de toutes les Troupes Françaises du Royaume au 15 mai 1758," Archives de la Guerre, Series A² (Papiers de Clermont), Volume 37, Manuscript no. 143. Since almost all the manuscript sources used in this work are from the Archives de Guerre the source will henceforth be cited simply by series (A¹, A², Mémoires Historiques), volume, and manuscript number, e.g. A² 37–143.

in June of that year. In 1757 France fielded two armies. The Army of the Lower Rhine, 99,000 men strong, was confided to Marshal d'Estrées, who began his march toward Hanover, defended by Cumberland. An auxiliary army of 24,000 was sent under the command of the Prince of Soubise to serve with the Imperial Army in Franconia, in accordance with the Franco-Austrian Treaty of May, 1756. D'Estrées crossed the Weser and defeated Cumberland at Hastenbeck (July 25). Marshal Richelieu replaced D'Estrées immediately afterward, penetrated into Hanover, and compelled Cumberland to sign the famous capitulation of Closter-Zeven (September 8). Versailles had hardly finished celebrating these victories, however, when fresh news came to change the picture radically. On November 5 Soubise and the Imperial Army were routed by Frederick at Rosbach; Ferdinand of Brunswick, who had succeeded Cumberland, suddenly renounced the Closter-Zeven agreement and recommenced operations (November 28). Richelieu was replaced by the Count of Clermont, who led the army in a long retreat back across the Rhine. Here he was defeated by Ferdinand at Krefeldt (June 23, 1758), and command of the Army of the Lower Rhine was then given to General Contades. Contades, in conjunction with Soubise, who commanded the smaller Army of the Upper Rhine, was able to drive Ferdinand back across the Rhine. Soubise penetrated briefly into Hanover and won a minor engagement over an allied detachment at Sondershausen (October 9). In November the French armies withdrew to quarters behind the Rhine, Meuse, and Neckar rivers.

When the campaign of 1759 opened in April Contades was given general command of both armies, the smaller being led by Marshal Broglie. After an initial victory by Broglie at Bergen (April 13), Ferdinand defeated Contades at Minden on the Weser (August 1) and the French were obliged to abandon Hesse and Westphalia. When the campaign of 1760 opened in May, Broglie had replaced Contades. Broglie won

The French Armies in the
Seven Years' War

1

The Central Authority

The elusive character of Louis XV has intrigued historians for two centuries; he was equally puzzling to his contemporaries who tried unsuccessfully to fathom his nature, and ended by calling him "impenetrable." [1] Whether motivated by indolence, timidity, boredom, or perhaps a compound of these, the king had long ceased to apply himself seriously to the tasks his august predecessor had called *"le métier du roi."* In 1756 his fateful liaison with the Marquise de Pompadour had already endured for a decade and would last another eight years. The blasé King and his mistress had embarked on their endless search for diversion. They regaled themselves by reading excerpts of letters opened by M. Janelle, head of the postal service.[2] Louis took a sly pleasure in carrying on "little private correspondences," the infamous *secret du roi.*[3] The King's chief passion, however, was hunting. The lawyer Barbier wrote in his diary during the critical summer of 1760: "The King makes one or two trips every week to Saint-Hubert, to Choisy, or to Bellevue, and all for the chase." [4]

Louis did not completely abdicate his official functions, but he fulfilled them with a singular lack of enthusiasm. His role in

1. Mouffle d'Angerville, *Vie privée de Louis XV ou principaux événemens, particularités et anecdotes de son règne* (London, 1781), III, 5.
2. Comte Jean-Nicolas Dufort de Cheverny, *Mémoires* (Paris, 1909), I, 287.
3. Madame Nicolle du Hausset, *Madame de Pompadour d'après le journal de sa femme de chambre* (Paris, 1910), p. 139.
4. E.-J.-F. Barbier, *Chronique de la régence et du règne de Louis XV (1718–1763); ou journal de Barbier* (Paris, 1857), VII, 263. There is perhaps no more eloquent testimony of royal dereliction than the records of the *petite meute*, Louis' pack of hunting dogs. During the war years they took 947 stags. Barbier, p. 77, n. 1.

the Conseil du Roi, the supreme organ of state, was more often that of spectator than active participant. The Abbé de Broglie complained of his sovereign in 1760: "He says 'Amen' to his ill-composed council; he would do better to say *Abrenuntio Satana.*"[5]

A series of minutes of council meetings toward the end of the war reveal how little initiative the King displayed. On Sunday, March 2, 1760, the council discussed the need of sending reinforcements to Martinique, but arrived at no decision. Two weeks later the minister of marine asked for twelve million livres to carry out the enterprise. The controller-general of finances pleaded lack of funds, and suggested a pro-rata cut in the budgets of the various ministries to provide the amount. At this point the minister of war objected strenuously to contributing his five million, though he felt he might be able to spare one million toward the end of the year. On March 31 the King suggested that the proposed expenditure be cut to five million livres, and appointed a committee of council members to settle a pro-rata contribution from each ministry. The committee could not reach agreement, and at the meeting of April 6 nothing was resolved. The whole question was then pushed into the background by more pressing matters, and when the relief expedition finally sailed for Martinique in 1762, the island had fallen to the English.[6]

The official correspondence that passed between the court and the armies bears little impress of the royal will. Only rarely could Louis be induced to write to his generals to fortify their resolution.[7] Occasionally, as he sat listening to a long dispatch from one of his armies, the sovereign would nod in agreement over some minor occurrence, and his reaction

5. Letter of the Abbé de Broglie to Marshal Broglie, June 5, 1760, as found in Albert, duc de Broglie, *Le secret du roi (1752–74)* (Paris, 1876), I, 385.

6. "Conseils des ministres sous Louis XV," *Revue rétrospective*, Ser. 3, III (1838), 343–72.

7. Thus he wrote to the Count of Clermont that further retreat would be "a mortal blow" to his policies. Letter of Feb. 26, 1758, A² 35–81.

would be faithfully recorded when the dispatch was answered: "His Majesty has strongly approved the conduct of the sergeant who fired on M. de Mazarin's servant." [8]

Louis' failure to play effectively the role allotted him had limitless ramifications. With the keystone defective the entire edifice built around it became disjointed. On the ministerial level the burden of government increased heavily. An astute political observer like Frederick the Great could detect all the evil consequences of the dislocation:

> The king wanted to work directly with his ministers. . . . His zeal was extinguished within a few days, and France was governed by four subaltern kings, each independent of the other. This mixed government could produce departmental details, but the general view which united and embraced "en grand" the welfare of the state and its interest, this was lacking in the councils. . . . This areopagus, then, governed France; it was in truth an aristocracy, or perhaps a vessel sailing without a compass on a stormy sea, simply following the impulsion of the winds.[9]

The French historian De Nolhac remarks that the somber years of Louis XV were one of the few difficult periods in the history of France in which no superior men arose to restore the nation's fortunes.[10] Among the many ministers of the period one searches in vain for men of the caliber of the elder Pitt or of Frederick II. The most likely candidate would be the Duke of Choiseul, but he dominated the cabinet only in 1761, when the war was already lost. Though his talents were indisputable, they were not equal to his ambition; he assumed the heavy burden of military, naval, and foreign affairs, but was never able to control finances, and thus never attained the commanding position of *premier ministre*.[11] For the rest of the conflict the ministries were held by men

8. Marshal Belle-Isle to General Contades, July 26, 1759, A¹ 3519–148.
9. Frederick II, *Histoire de mon temps* (*Œuvres posthumes* [Berlin, 1788]), II, 6–7.
10. Pierre de Nolhac, *Madame de Pompadour et la politique d'après des documents nouveaux* (Paris, 1928), p. 262.
11. There is no adequate study of Choiseul. The work usually cited is that of Gaston Maugras, *Le duc et la duchesse de Choiseul* (Paris, 1902).

unable to divorce themselves from the factions and intrigues that brought them in and out of power.

The minister of war in 1756 was the able Marquis d'Argenson, who had been in office since 1743. He was dismissed in disgrace in February, 1757, shortly after the Damiens affair. His successor was his nephew, the Marquis de Paulmy. This young man had gained experience working in his uncle's ministry, but his meager talents and timid nature made him little more than a "signature machine." [12] Paulmy was replaced by Marshal Belle-Isle in March, 1758, and it was hoped that with the post in the hands of a professional soldier for the first time, the nation's military fortunes might improve. Belle-Isle did indeed possess an illustrious record in the army, but his background was a mixed blessing; he always had difficulty distinguishing the functions of a minister from those of a general; what is more he was now a semi-invalid of seventy-three who hobbled about with a cane and endured the torments of erysipelas, sciatica, and old battle wounds.[13] At his death in January, 1761, his ministry was assumed by Choiseul.

If the ministries were undistinguished they were also ephemeral, and here lies a second weakness of Louis XV's government. President Hénault noted with a touch of humor that ministers changed like the scenery at the opera.[14] There were four ministers of foreign affairs during the war, and five ministers of marine. The thankless office of controller-general of finances was occupied by a monotonous succession of appointees, illuminated only by the brief, spectacular, and ill-starred career of the famous M. de Silhouette.[15]

12. Xavier Audouin, *Histoire de l'administration de la guerre* (Paris, 1811), III, 6.
13. Dussauge, *Etudes*, p. 87.
14. President Charles-Jean-François Hénault, *Mémoires* (Paris, 1855), p. 199.
15. The ministers of foreign affairs were: Antoine-Louis Rouillé to June, 1757; Abbé de Bernis to December, 1758; Duc de Choiseul to October, 1761; Duc de Praslin to April, 1766. The ministers of marine: Machault d'Arnouville to February, 1757; Peirenc de Moras to May, 1758;

In theory power lay in the Crown and by delegation in public functionaries who aided the monarch, but it would be a serious error to assume that under the old regime the holder of an office always exercised its functions. In practice the reign of Louis XV was distinguished by the fact that authority was often diverted from the prescribed channels, to be concentrated in the hands of individuals who had no official position within the central hierarchy. Easily the most celebrated of these, and perhaps the most misunderstood, was Jeanne le Normant, marquise de Pompadour. Her numerous enemies laid all the ills of the country at her door, and created the image of the sinister *éminence grise,* the "minister more powerful than the king." [16] The French historian De Nolhac was still under the influence of this myth some thirty-five years ago when he began his exhaustive study of the famous courtesan. As his research progressed, he found the customary interpretation unsupported by fact:

> In reality . . . she directed nothing in the important decisions of Louis XV and his ministers. But since she was involved in many matters, and informed of nearly all, since the King made daily use of her devotion and her feminine mind, and since she was powerful in nominations and in the disgraces, her role remains one of lively interest and merits exposition in detail.[17]

The part played by the Marquise in the war bears out De Nolhac's conclusions. She did have an influence on the choice of commanders as will be seen, but even here her will did not always prevail. She unquestionably favored a vigorous prosecution of the war, but her lack of knowledge in such matters enabled the stronger ministers to dominate her.[18] In the actual

---

Marquis de Massiac to November, 1758; Nicolas-René Berryer to October, 1761; Duc de Choiseul to April, 1766. The controllers-general: Peirenc de Moras to August, 1757; Jean de Boullongne to March, 1759; Etienne de Silhouette to November, 1759; Henri-Lionard-Jean-Baptiste Bertin to December, 1763.

16. Audouin, *Administration,* III, 5.
17. De Nolhac, *Pompadour,* pp. 350–51.
18. *Ibid.,* pp. 300–303; Mouffle d'Angerville, *Louis XV,* IV, 23.

conduct of operations there is no evidence of her direct influence or intervention. She carried on a lively correspondence with several commanders, but the letters which survive are largely filled with mutual expressions of devotion and plans for finding sinecures for friends and relations.[19]

Among the individuals who played a role in the conduct of the war, the court bankers deserve an important place. It was they who made the war financially possible by coming to the rescue of the hard-pressed controller-general. The financier Paris de Montmartel and his brother, Paris Duverney, formed an invincible partnership, the one supplying money and the other controlling the provisioning of the armies. The history of the Paris family is an eighteenth-century success story; the brothers, originally four, began life as sons of an obscure Dauphiné tavernkeeper and founded their fortunes supplying bread to the armies of Louis XIV during the War of the Spanish Succession. They had first tasted political power when they were charged with clearing away the debris of the Mississippi Bubble.

Paris Duverney had a decisive voice in the conduct of the war. His brother's indispensable wealth, his own experience, and his close friendship with Madame de Pompadour enabled him to usurp a large part of the war ministry's functions. Not content with arrogating to himself all problems of supply, the querulous old man expounded his own views on military operations.[20] The ministers were obliged to tolerate this

19. Clermont's papers, the A² series, contain a score of her letters. The great bulk of her correspondence has been lost, but is often alluded to: "Madame de Pompadour me marque beaucoup de bontés; j'ai l'honneur de lui écrire par touts les couriers que j'envoye." Contades to Marquis de Castries, Aug. 6, 1758, A¹ 3480–78.

20. His numerous memoranda on operations are found in the A¹ series. His influence in this regard can also be found throughout his published correspondence: *Correspondance particulière du comte de Saint Germain avec M. Paris Duverney* (2 vols., London, 1789); *Correspondance particulière et historique du maréchal duc de Richelieu en 1756, 1757 et 1758 avec M. Paris Duverney* (2 vols., London, 1789). Mme du Hausset goes so far as to attribute to him the plan of campaign for 1757, but there is no corroboration for this. Du Hausset, *Journal*, pp. 139–40.

"General of the Flour Bags," and to cajole him into returning to his functions when fits of pique drove him to brooding
retreat at "Plaisance," his country villa.[21]
The displacement of responsibility was sometimes so widespread that it produced a sort of "shadow" government. This
bizarre situation existed in 1757. The Minister of War was
Paulmy, but military affairs were in the hands of a trium-
virate—Belle-Isle, Paris Duverney, and Marshal d'Estrées.
There was a minister of foreign affairs, Rouillé, but policy
was being formulated by Bernis. There was a controller-general of finances, Peirenc de Moras, but his functions were
being fulfilled by Paris de Montmartel.

To this dispersion of authority must be added the friction
and quarreling which rent the government and cost it its
harmony. The *enjambements,* incursions by one minister into
the jurisdiction of another, were frequent. Marshal d'Estrées
was relieved of command by means of a cabal to which the
minister of war was not a party.[22] In 1760 Louis and Belle-Isle
sent the Count of Saint Germain to the Hague to discuss
peace terms, and the mission was carefully concealed from
Choiseul, then minister of foreign affairs.[23]

The picture which emerges is that of a government of
personalities, with the stronger dominating the weaker and
decisions being made by alliances of interest. The official
records seldom reveal the hidden springs which governed the
operation of the governmental machinery. All too often the

21. "Lorsque Duverney partait pour Plaisance, la caisse de Montmartel
se fermait, et lorsque la caisse de Montmartel se fermait, le contrôleur
général ne savait plus comment fournir à la dépense." Camille Rousset, *Le
comte de Gisors, 1732–1758* (Paris, 1868), p. 153.
22. *Ibid.,* pp. 236–43.
23. G. P. Gooch, *Louis XV: The Monarchy in Decline* (London, 1956),
p. 212; see also the letter of Ferdinand of Brunswick to Frederick dated
April 2, 1760, in Christian Heinrich Phillip Edler von Westphalen,
*Geschichte der Feldzüge des Herzogs Ferdinand von Braunschweig-
Lüneburg* (Berlin, 1859–1872), IV, 211. The Count of Saint Germain
referred to here was the eccentric adventurer who figures in Casanova's
Mémoires. He was not related to Claude-Louis, Count of Saint Germain,
the general who will be mentioned subsequently.

researcher can only catch a glimpse of these intimate scenes in which the fate of the nation was decided: The King is starting out on one of his innumerable hunts when the minister of war rushes out and stops the royal carriage in the courtyard. There follows five minutes of agitated conversation—a conversation lost to history.[24] Marshal Soubise begins a letter to his friend: "I am writing to you with M. de Choiseul at Madame de Pompadour's table . . . ," yet he says nothing of the deliberations of these three powerful figures.[25] One evening Bernis, Paris Duverney, and General Crémilles gather in Belle-Isle's *cabinet de travail;* a few days later the Army of the Lower Rhine has a new commander.[26]

The governing coalition could provide no continuity of policy, because that coalition was always ephemeral. The constantly shifting power relationships were byzantine in their complexity. The historian dissects them in vain, for they possessed no more logic than permanence. In the words of a contemporary, all was "moving sand." [27]

The ministry of war merits close examination, since it was the agency chiefly charged with the conduct of the war. Since the days of LeTellier and Louvois the holder of this post was one of the chief officers of the realm.[28] The minister of war held a place in the Conseil du Roi, and in addition he had the right of direct consultation to the monarch concerning affairs in his department, or as the expression was, he could "take the orders of His Majesty." He countersigned the royal *ordonnances* which governed the military establishment. Through the minister's hands passed almost all the official

24. Charles-Philippe-Albert, duc de Luynes, *Mémoires sur la cour de Louis XV (1735–1758)* (Paris, 1860–1865), XVII, 470.
25. Soubise to Castries, April 16, 1759, A¹ 3514–144.
26. See Paris Duverney's "Notes" of June 22 and 24, 1758, A² 38–89, 90.
27. Hénault, *Mémoires,* p. 214.
28. The official title of the minister of war was *Ministre et secrétaire d'état ayant le département de la guerre.* His salary was about 80,000 livres per annum in addition to other emoluments, such as a forage allotment of 3,000 livres annually. Hélion, vicomte de Luçay, *Des origines du pouvoir ministériel en France. Les secrétaires d'état depuis leur institution jusqu'à la mort de Louis XV* (Paris, 1881), p. 484; Dussauge, *Etudes,* p. 102.

correspondence between court and army.[29] His competence covered the following matters: the standing army,
the militia, coastal defense, the Ecole Militaire, the Invalides,
the *haras* or royal stud farms, and the *Maréchaussée*. In
addition the ministry was charged with the collection of the
taillon or supplementary *taille,* and with the administration
of the frontier provinces and *généralités:* the "Three Bis-
hoprics" (Metz, Toul, and Verdun), Le Barrois, Artois,
Flandre, Hainault, Alsace, Franche-Comté, Roussillon, Dauphiné, and the town of Sedan with its dependencies.[30]

By tradition the work of the ministry was divided into
bureaus, along lines that would seem rather irrational to the
modern administrator. They were: (1) provisions, discipline,
and military correspondence (by far the most important
bureau); (2) nominations, vacancies, decorations, and pensions; (3) troop movements, particularly their marches or
étapes; (4) pay, pensions, gratifications, and brevets; (5)
details of officers' salaries and infractions of military justice;
(6) expedition of royal orders and *arrêts*; (7) artillery, fortifications, *Maréchaussée,* food, and forage; and (8) militia,
hospitals, uniforms, and "bed, wood, and candle"—the three
facilities accorded to troops in winter quarters.[31]

It is somewhat paradoxical that the agency charged with
the military establishment of a nation of twenty million should
be so incredibly small. The minister could sometimes reduce
the staggering burden of business by employing an *adjoint* or

29. The sanctity of "channels" was already a well established feature of
the military hierarchy. When the Count of Lusace wrote a letter of thanks
to Louis for his commission as lieutenant general, he apologized to Belle-
Isle: "Vous ne trouverez pas mauvais que je sois un peu sorti des règles pour
l'en remercier." Lusace to Belle-Isle, Aug. 23, 1758, A¹ 3481–111.

30. *Almanach royal de 1758* (Paris, 1758), p. 96.

31. Commandant Jean-Lambert-Alphonse Colin, *Les campagnes du
maréchal de Saxe* (Paris, 1901–1904), I, 136. Choiseul reorganized the
bureaus along more logical lines. In 1771 the seven bureaus were:
(1) gratifications, pensions, commissions, and leaves; (2) routes, troop
movements, remounts, and militia; (3) artillery, fortifications, engineers; (4)
official correspondence; (5) clothing and equipment; (6) archives; and (7)
subsistence. Luçay, *Secrétaires d'état,* pp. 484–85.

assistant. D'Argenson employed Paulmy in this capacity, and Belle-Isle was similarly aided by General Crémilles. As a rule Belle-Isle corresponded with the field commanders on military operations; Crémilles—and the ubiquitous Paris Duverney— took charge of logistical matters and the correspondence with the intendants of the armies. A dozen *commis* and a battery of copy clerks completed the ministerial personnel. Notations on incoming dispatches indicate that they were often referred to the *commis* who prepared rough drafts of the replies, which then went out under the signature of the minister or of his *adjoint*.³² The hundreds of marginal notations on these drafts written in Belle-Isle's trembling hand indicate to what degree the minister personally supervised the work of his assistants. The amount of paper work was enormous. The official correspondence with the armies in Germany alone fills twenty large volumes for the year 1760—some five thousand pieces. To this must be added the interministerial memoranda and a voluminous correspondence concerning coastal defense and the colonial war. Belle-Isle was probably not exaggerating when he confided that he worked fifteen hours a day.³³

The rather casual organization of the ministry is reflected in its makeshift quarters. For the greater part of the war there was no ministry building. The minister worked in his Paris residence or at Versailles; the bureaus were installed in private houses near the royal palace, rented at exorbitant rates. Here the *commis* and clerks sat on stools, sorting their papers on crude tables—a few planks stretched over pairs of barrels.³⁴

The *dépôt* or archives were kept at the Invalides, as were

32. The names of the *commis* which appear in the notations of referral are nine: MM. Fumeron, Segent *père,* Segent *fils,* Le Tourneur, Saint Laurent, Patiot, Des Prez, Blondeau, and Thibault. In 1771 the total expenses of the bureaus, including the salaries of the *commis,* were only 149,000 livres. Luçay, *Secrétaires d'état,* p. 485.

33. Belle-Isle to Paris Duverney, July 11, 1758, Aª 38–162. It should be borne in mind that Choiseul held this ministry and two others in 1761.

34. Paul Laurencin-Chapelle, *Les archives de guerre historiques et administratives, 1688–1898* (Paris, 1898), p. 20; Audouin, *Administration,* III, 233.

the map collections of the corps of *ingénieurs-géographes.*[35]
During the war the government built a structure at Versailles
for all of the ministry's services, but it was not ready for oc-
cupancy until 1761.[36]

This then was the government of Louis XV and more
particularly the agency through which it directed and administered its armies during the Seven Years' War. The
extreme importance of this central authority will become clear
with an examination of the concept of command.

35. During most of the seventeenth century the ministers had kept their
documents in their homes. Louvois found his house so encumbered with this
accretion that he had it transferred to the attics of Versailles. When Louis
XIV learned that he was sleeping with this mass of highly inflammable
paper over his head, he gave orders for its removal to the Invalides.
Audouin, *Administration,* III, 234.

36. Luçay, *Secrétaires d'état,* p. 481.

2

Command

It might be well to begin the study of field command by examining in detail the process by which the leaders were selected—a factor which greatly colored their role. The formal designation of command was made by the King. The general who received his letter of appointment found in it the customary expression of royal confidence in his abilities; but the selection was really the result of subterranean maneuverings at court in which the appointee himself was usually deeply involved. Perhaps an exception could be made in the appointment of the highly regarded Marshal d'Estrées in 1757, though at least one author attributes his selection to the efforts of Belle-Isle.[1] There seems little doubt that the auxiliary army was given by Pompadour to "son cher Soubise."[2]

During the summer of 1757 there was much complaint over the slowness of D'Estrées' advance.[3] In truth, the blame could not be placed at the general's door, for his movements were hamstrung by a faulty system of supply. When he pointed this out by way of justification, he incurred the wrath of Paris Duverney. Characteristically Duverney denied responsibility and threatened to retire.[4] D'Estrées was already

1. Rousset, *Gisors,* p. 144.
2. Charles de Rohan, Prince of Soubise. Unfortunately, this extremely influential figure has never been the subject of a monograph; for his importance and his relations with Louis XV and the Marquise, see General Charles-François Dumouriez, *Galérie des aristocrates militaires et mémoires secrets* (London, 1790), pp. 117–31; and Michaud's *Biographie universelle* (2nd ed., Paris, 1843), XXXIX, 661–64.
3. Mouffle d'Angerville, *Louis XV,* III, 123; Chevalier de Ray, *Réflexions et souvenirs* (Paris and Limoges, 1895), p. 103.
4. Paris Duverney to D'Estrées, May 27, 1757, A³ 34–58.

on bad terms with Paulmy, then minister of war,[5] and the estrangement of Paris Duverney proved fatal. By July D'Estrées' enemies had enough support to obtain his replacement by Marshal Richelieu. The victory rebounded to the discredit of the cabal, however; the letter of recall arrived on July 30, just four days after D'Estrées' victory at Hastenbeck.[6] D'Estrées' successor owed his appointment to his earlier conquest of Minorca and to a carefully cultivated friendship with Duverney and Bernis.[7] These advantages for a time outweighed the enmity of Madame de Pompadour and Belle-Isle.[8] Richelieu's chief accomplishment, the capitulation of Closter-Zeven, proved abortive, and by the end of the year his laurels were severely tarnished. Like D'Estrées, he became involved in a bitter dispute with Paris Duverney over the failings of the supply system. The course of their quarrels is faithfully mirrored in their correspondence. By September the irascible "Flour Bag General" was again threatening to retire—a distinct danger sign [9]—and Richelieu had adopted an attitude

5. D'Estrées referred to Paulmy as "cet excrément de Paulmy," an epithet which duly made the rounds of the court. Charles Duclos, *Mémoires secrets sur le règne de Louis XIV, la régence et le règne de Louis XV* (Paris, 1864), II, 287.
6. For details of the conspiracy see Rousset, *Gisors*, pp. 236–43. The illtimed recall inspired numerous satirical verses, one of which was particularly telling:

> Nous avons deux généraux
> Qui tous deux sont Maréchaux,
> Voilà la ressemblance.
> L'un de Mars est le favori,
> Et l'autre l'est de Louis,
> Voilà la différence.
> —Mouffle d'Angerville, *Louis XV*, III, 330.

7. At the time of his nomination Richelieu lavished flattery on Duverney: "C'est de vous seul, et avec vous seul, que je pourrais travailler et recevoir les lumières nécessaires pour un si grand ouvrage." Undated letter in *Correspondance Richelieu–Paris Duverney*, I, 110. For Richelieu's relations with Bernis, see *Mémoires authentiques du Maréchal de Richelieu (1725–1757)* (Paris, 1918), pp. 149–61.
8. Richelieu apparently regarded Belle-Isle as his chief enemy: "Ce misérable Maréchal de Belle-Isle . . . me désole au milieu de ce conseil où l'on ne m'entend point, et où je n'essuie que tracasseries." Richelieu to Paris Duverney, Oct. 30, 1757, *Correspondance Richelieu–Paris Duverney*, II, 4.
9. Paris Duverney to Richelieu, Sept. 7, 1757, *ibid.*, I, 159.

of injured dignity.[10] By December Paris Duverney had abandoned his protegé, and with consummate guile warned him: "If, moreover, you are informed of what is transpiring here, you should know that I am not without apprehension regarding you yourself." [11]

In January, 1758, the Army of the Lower Rhine received its third commander in less than a year—the Count of Clermont. This bizarre figure led a double life; he was the Abbé of Saint Germain-des-Prés, but a papal dispensation had enabled him to embark on a military career as well.[12] Clermont owed his appointment less to powerful connections than to his high birth (he was a great-grandson of the great Condé), and to his incessant clamoring for a command. As soon as hostilities began he sent a memoir to Louis in which he pointed out that he had made nine campaigns, and during the years of peace he "had not ceased to study the theory of war." [13] When D'Estrées was given command in 1757, not even Madame de Pompadour was spared the explosion of Clermont's indignation:

> Count d'Estrées is detested by the troops, and I am loved and esteemed by them. . . . They say aloud that I could lead them into hell and they would go with pleasure, but with Count d'Estrées they will do their duty, for a Frenchman could do nothing else, but they will do it with death in their souls.[14]

Clermont retained command for only six months, during which time his incompetence was made manifest. The Count of Gisors wrote an anguished letter to his father, Belle-Isle, concerning the new general's incapacity: Clermont was in-

10. See especially his letter to Paris Duverney of Sept. 7, 1757, *ibid.*, I, 174–75.

11. Paris Duverney to Richelieu, Dec. 18, 1757, *ibid.*, II, 16–17.

12. The slightly ridiculous figure of the "Benedictine General" was the butt of endless jests. He has been the subject of a biography, J. Cousin, *Le comte de Clermont et ses amis* (Paris, 1867); but the best picture of him is to be found in his own correspondence, the A² series in the Archives de la Guerre.

13. Memoir of Sept. 17, 1756, A² 34–15.

14. Clermont to Pompadour, March 3, 1757, A² 34–21.

capable of forming any project himself, but adopted the view of whoever had spoken to him last. "He foresees nothing and is unaffected by the present danger. . . . He wastes his time with useless promenades." [15] After his defeat at Krefeldt he was recalled, angrily protesting that though betrayed by his subordinates, he had nonetheless conducted an "audacious and glorious retreat." [16]

The task of choosing a new commander proved a difficult one. Bernis and Belle-Isle preferred to reinstate D'Estrées, while Paris Duverney and Crémilles favored the Count of Saint Germain. Finally the deadlock was resolved by simply appointing the ranking lieutenant general serving with the army—the Marquis de Contades.[17] Contades was almost an unknown (Captain Mercoyrol de Beaulieu, a career officer since 1743, had never heard of the new general until the day of his appointment).[18] To enhance his prestige, Contades was given the marshal's baton as soon as he had maneuvered Ferdinand back across the Rhine.[19] One of Contades' fellow officers commented: "One can't do too much to give him the dignity and authority of which in truth he has great need." [20]

Contades was able to retain command until 1759. During that year a serious rival arose, Marshal Broglie. The competition between the two men came to a head at the unfortunate battle of Minden, where Broglie commanded a detachment under Contades. Contades blamed the defeat on Broglie's failure to second him effectively, and the hot-tempered Broglie angrily denied the charge.[21] The controversy was aired in Council, where Belle-Isle, D'Estrées, and Soubise

15. Gisors to Belle-Isle, June 18, 1758, A² 3477–37.
16. Clermont to Belle-Isle, July 6, 1758, A¹ 3487–156.
17. Mouffle d'Angerville, *Louis XV*, IV, 24.
18. Jacques Mercoyrol de Beaulieu, *Campagnes 1743–1763* (Paris, 1915), p. 195.
19. He owed this favor chiefly to Belle-Isle and Madame de Pompadour. See letter of Contades to Marquis de Castries, Aug. 29, 1758, A¹ 3481–199.
20. General Chevert to Belle-Isle, Aug. 27, 1758, A¹ 3481–154.
21. Broglie to Belle-Isle, Aug. 3, 1759, A¹ 3520–12. See also M. de Plainchamp's letter to Belle-Isle of Aug. 1, 1759, A¹ 3520–8; and Mercoyrol de Beaulieu, *Campagnes*, p. 251.

supported Contades.[22] For all his faults, Broglie was an able general. His powerful family seconded his ambitions through their ties with the royal family; morning and evening the Abbé de Broglie could be seen hurrying about the royal palace in his nephew's behalf.[23]

Broglie assumed command and retained it for two years, during which time his enemies did not abandon the struggle.[24] The campaign of 1761 called for co-operation between the two armies commanded by Broglie and Soubise. Their defeat at Fillingshausen began a fierce debate between them and their partisans over the responsibility for the reverse. Broglie knew that in attacking Soubise he was attacking the Marquise, so he took the unusual step of presenting a memoir justifying his conduct to the King. The royal reply was a thunderbolt:

> My cousin, having judged that the form and spirit of your action in presenting me a memoir on the events of the last campaign were contrary to the good of my service as well as a bad example in my kingdom, I am signifying to you my displeasure by depriving you of the command of my province of Alsace and ordering you to leave for your estate of Broglie on Saturday, where you will remain until further order.[25]

The final campaign of the war is only a postscript. The command of the army was given not to one general but two—

22. Belle-Isle to Contades (*lettre particulière*), Aug. 12, 1759, A¹ 3520–159.

23. Broglie, *Secret,* I, 340, 375.

24. Ferdinand of Brunswick's agent at the Hague reported in 1760: "M. de Soubise, qui ne fait que sottise, remue ciel et terre pour avoir le commandement de l'armée de Broglie. Ou d'une autre de pareille force." Letter of M. Haenichen to von Westphalen, Jan. 16, 1760, in Westphalen, *Feldzüge,* IV, 79. Broglie's most dangerous enemy was Belle-Isle. The enmity between the two families was one which "neither time nor death could extinguish." Broglie, *Secret,* I, 307.

25. This letter of February 17 is reproduced in Ray, *Réflexions,* p. 372. The sacrifice of this popular general was not without disturbing repercussions. At the time of his disgrace the Comédie Française was presenting Voltaire's *Tancrède.* When the celebrated actress Mlle Clairon recited with obvious emphasis the lines: "On dépouille Tancrède, on l'exile, on l'outrage," the inference was clear and the play was interrupted by a tremendous outburst of applause. Mouffle d'Angerville, *Louis XV,* III, 136; Hénault, *Mémoires,* p. 285.

D'Estrées and Soubise. The original plan had been to give the army to the inept Soubise, but public outcry was so great that D'Estrées was added.[26] As has already been noted, by this time diplomatic activity was of increasing importance, and the end of hostilities saved the army from the disaster that this experiment in dual command seemed to promise.

Once a general was installed in a position of command by the devious means just described, what precisely was his function? Like so many other aspects of the French military establishment, the concept of command was a legacy of the era of Louis XIV. Under that strong-willed monarch the direction of the war machine had been highly centralized. The levers of control were installed at Versailles to the utmost point of feasibility—and sometimes beyond. The Marquis de Chamlay, the Sun King's military conscience, saw nothing but advantage in the system. Previously the fortunes of the monarchy had been dependent on the ability of a Turenne or a Condé, but with the new arrangement "the king finds himself able to have his army commanded by whomever he wishes, without any need for apprehension about the mediocre capacity of those to whom it is confided." [27] Thus talent and initiative were deemed superfluous, and obedience became the hallmark of the good field commander. This arrangement continued unaltered under Louis XV. Even the most head-strong of his commanders, Marshal Broglie, wrote to the court in 1759: "I have no will, and I am ready to do all that may be prescribed to me." [28]

The conclusion frequently drawn was that the field commander merely executed decisions made at Versailles, with every movement being determined at court. This view was

26. Hénault, *Mémoires,* p. 285. A fellow officer described this experiment in dual command in these terms: "Ces deux têtes dans un même bonnet ne valait pas une bonne." General Pierre-Joseph de Bourcet, *Mémoires historiques sur la guerre que les Français ont soutenu en Allemagne depuis 1757 jusqu'en 1762* (Paris, 1792), *discours préliminaire,* p. xv.

27. Quoted by Emile G. Léonard, *L'Armée et ses problèmes au XVIII° siècle* (Paris, 1958), p. 10.

28. Broglie to Belle-Isle, March 10, 1759, A¹ 3513–86.

even accepted by many in the army itself.[29] Two very practical considerations ruled out such an arrangement. Distance and slow communications made it virtually impossible for Versailles to receive dispatches and have its replies reach the army without a time lapse of at least a week. Then too, the impetus frequently came from the enemy; Ferdinand with his smaller army was often able to hold the initiative, much to the chagrin of the French court.[30]

In theory, at least, the field commander had a large degree of tactical latitude. The court provided the plan of campaign, with an outline of the means and objectives. Within this framework the general was to be his own master. The minister of war himself confirmed this view:

> It is certain that the general must be the master of his movements. I know more than anyone else that one cannot command an army from Versailles. All that the minister can and should do is to make known to the general the political and military objectives and the King's manner of thinking.[31]

In 1760 the same minister gave Broglie a complete *carte blanche* for the conduct of operations.[32]

The discretion which Versailles accorded in principle, it curtailed in detail. The field commander had the uneasy knowledge that his every movement was being traced on the maps at court and subjected to the criticism of fellow officers

---

29. It was widely but erroneously held that Contades fought at Minden on express order of the court. Mercoyrol de Beaulieu, *Campagnes*, p. 218; Ray, *Réflexions*, p. 131; captured letter of M. Castilla dated Aug. 3, 1759, in Westphalen, *Feldzüge*, III, 549.

30. "Et ce qui peine le plus le Roi, est de voir dans toutes vos lettres, que vous êtes redevenu si décisivement aux ordres du Prince Ferdinand, que vous répétez toujours dans toutes vos lettres que vous attendez d'être instruit de ses mouvements pour régler les vôtres." Belle-Isle to Contades, Sept. 17, 1758, A¹ 3483–78.

31. Belle-Isle to Contades, July 23, 1758, A¹ 3479–157.

32. "Le Roy vous laisse donc, M. le Maréchal, le maître absolu de prendre le parti que vous proposez, ou tel autre que vous jugerez le plus praticable et le plus utile pour le bien de son service, celuy de la cause commune et la gloire de ses armes." Belle-Isle to Broglie, June 6, 1760, A¹ 3555–81.

who coveted his command.[33] The minister's letters are full of orders masquerading as suggestions. France needs a victorious battle, the minister explains: "I cannot repeat this too often. The King will never order it, but he thinks of it and desires it." [34] Sometimes the "suggestions" were contradictory: on one occasion Belle-Isle was pressing Soubise to advance and Paris Duverney was urging him to remain where he was.[35]

The ministerial intervention had its negative aspect in the thinly veiled criticisms of the commander's conduct. Why had he not occupied the camp at Dulmen, since "those who know the region" think it advisable? [36] Was it true that he had abandoned his field hospital to the enemy? [37] Why did the troops march fifteen leagues in moving from Wolfhagen to Marburg when the map showed a more direct route? [38] The commander took great pains to refute these criticisms, lest they provide a fulcrum with which his enemies could dislodge him from his post.

These were the usual methods by which the government fettered the leaders of its armies. When the campaign was not going well or when there was a disagreement between the court and the commander, the exhortations became more strident, the King's "manner of thinking" more explicit. Sometimes the impatience and dissatisfaction of Versailles led it even to short-circuit the chain of command. On such occasions the court issued direct orders to subordinate commanders in the field, or even countermanded the orders of the general commanding; however, such instances were rare.[39]

33. When D'Estrées and Soubise were not in the field they took part in the deliberations of the Conseil du Roi.

34. Belle-Isle to General Mortaigne, June 13, 1758, A¹ 3476–185.

35. Belle-Isle to Soubise, Aug. 7, 1758, A¹ 3480–101; Paris Duverney to General de Vault, Aug. 7, 1758, A¹ 3480–92.

36. Belle-Isle to Contades, Sept. 19, 1758, A¹ 3483–78.

37. Belle-Isle to Broglie, April 27, 1759, A¹ 3514–238.

38. Belle-Isle to Broglie, Aug. 8, 1760, A¹ 3558–99.

39. In September, 1759, the court was sending direct orders to the commanders of garrisons on the Rhine. See Belle-Isle to Contades, Sept. 8, 1759, A¹ 3522–122. When Clermont ordered the evacuation of Emden and

Correspondence with the court took much of a general's time. He was obliged to write so frequently and in such detail that the practice was the subject of much ridicule. One evening when the Count of Clermont was entertaining some of his officers at dinner, he excused himself to write a dispatch to Versailles. After he had gone, one of the officers present remarked that he could not understand what his commander had to write about, since nothing had happened recently. Another officer, the witty Count of Saint Germain, replied:

> Let me tell you what he is writing: "I got up today at nine o'clock after having slept very well—indeed I even snored. At ten I made a reconnaissance in which I did not see anything. I returned to headquarters at eleven and had a shave; when my valet curled my wig, instead of beginning with the right side, as was usual, he began with the left side." The minister replies: "Your last dispatch, which is extremely interesting, has caused deep reflections here which it would be well to communicate to you. Why did you not get up at eight o'clock? You could have made the reconnaissance you mentioned at nine o'clock instead of ten, and you might have seen something. It is quite understandable that you had a shave, particularly if your beard was long: God grant that you were not nicked! But it is extraordinary that your valet ignored custom and began curling your wig on the left side. Since the King was surprised at this, you will be so good as to send me the reasons for it, so that I can report them to His Majesty, whose further intentions I will communicate to you." [40]

The general was spurred to his task by the knowledge that if he did not report an occurrence, the court would nevertheless receive an account of it—perhaps a more hostile one—from other sources. The ministers had their confidential correspondents with the army, and the reports of some of these spies are still to be found in the archives. One of them in particular, M. de Plainchamp, pursued his work with im-

---

Hanau in early 1758, the minister ordered the commanders of these places to hold them. Belle-Isle to Clermont, March 26, 1758, A¹ 3473–195; Belle-Isle to Comte de Lorges, March 23, 1758, A¹ 3473–169.

40. *Correspondance Saint Germain–Paris Duverney*, prefatory "Vie de Saint Germain," I, 16–17.

placable determination. The army's chief of staff reports on
June 11, 1759: "We have had a little desertion in the past
few days." [41] De Plainchamp writes on the same day: "During
the past several days desertion has become very great in our
troops." [42] Contades writes on June 13, "The army had just
arrived in its camp. . . . The march was long but well prepared and was not tiring for the troops." [43] De Plainchamp's
version was different: "Today's march was badly reconnoit-
ered; the columns were cut several times by the baggage
train." [44] A few days later Contades wrote: "There is still a
little desertion but it is diminishing." [45] "It is true that the
number of sick has increased but less than I feared." [46] De
Plainchamp went into embarrassing detail: "Six hundred
soldiers entered the hospitals today after a difficult march.
A thousand have deserted within the past ten or eleven days.
Bread is scarce and mouldy." [47]

The commander was further hindered in his operations
by the fact that his subordinates were frequently not of his
own choosing, and were often openly hostile to him. (Even
when the French forces were under single command, there
were always one or more important *réserves*—detached corps
with distinct though subordinate commands.) In 1757
D'Estrées was given General Maillebois as his chief of staff,
and Maillebois wrote dispatches to his brother-in-law, Paulmy,
which were openly critical of his superior.[48] Broglie asked
for the Chevalier de Muy as the ranking lieutenant general

41. General Cornillon to Belle-Isle, June 11, 1759, A¹ 3517–147.
42. Report of June 11, 1759, A¹ 3517–143.
43. Contades to Belle-Isle, June 13, 1759, A¹ 3517–174.
44. Report of June 13, 1759, A¹ 3517–173.
45. Contades to Belle-Isle, June 26, 1759, A¹ 3517–327.
46. Contades to Belle-Isle, June 27, 1759, A¹ 3517–343.
47. Report of June 25, 1759, A¹ 3517–317. Even the most minor
occurrences at headquarters were faithfully recorded by De Plainchamp:
"Le Mal. d'Estrées n'a pas monté aujourd' hui à cause d'un coup de pied du
cheval de M. de Pce. de Condé qu'il a reçu hier." Report of Sept. 20, 1759,
A¹ 3523–58.
48. See for example Maillebois' letter to Paulmy of June 14, 1757, A¹
3436–119.

in his army in 1760, but was given instead General Dumesnil, a creature of Paris Duverney.[49] Moreover the court, not Broglie, chose Saint Germain to command the *réserve*.[50]

The general commanding was so unsure of his authority and so afraid of alienating powerful interests at court that he seldom took action against incompetent or disloyal subordinates—though this was his prerogative. Both Richelieu and Clermont complained of the Duke of Randan, whom they considered "imbecilic," "extremely limited"; yet they looked to Versailles to rid them of his presence.[51] When Broglie dismissed Saint Germain—a *cause célèbre* in 1760— he did so with much trepidation. To justify his action he assembled all the lieutenant generals and read to them his correspondence with the vitriolic Saint Germain; even this did not extinguish the smouldering resentment of Saint Germain's partisans.[52]

A French officer lamented in 1758: "The camp is like the court: it is the seat of intrigues, jealousies, and bad faith." [53] Small wonder then that every reverse suffered by the French inevitably produced a storm of recrimination which swept the army and the court. The acrimonious debates that followed Minden and Fillingshausen have already been noted. The fruits of victory were likewise disputed. Broglie's partisans insisted that he had won at Bergen not because of the

49. The ranking lieutenant general took charge *ad interim* if the commander were incapacitated. The efforts of the Broglie clan to prevent Dumesnil's nomination to this post were typically devious. The Abbé de Broglie told the impressionable Dauphine that Dumesnil would certainly cause the loss of a battle, in which her brother might well be killed. Broglie, *Secret,* I, 401.

50. Louis Mention, *Le comte de Saint Germain et ses réformes* (Paris, 1884), Introduction, p. xix.

51. Richelieu to Paulmy, Dec. 23, 1757, A¹ 3446–29; Clermont to Belle-Isle, May 17, 1758, A¹ 3502–206.

52. Broglie to Louis XV, July 20, 1760, A¹ 3557–76. Several of Saint Germain's friends asked for their recall. See for example the Marquis de Voyer's letter to Belle-Isle of July 22, 1760, A¹ 3557–110. Comte du Luc asked for an indefinite leave on the pretext that his hemorrhoids made it impossible for him to mount horseback. M. Doriel to Belle-Isle, July 21, 1760, A¹ 3557–96.

53. Captured letter of M. Castella (no date), in Westphalen, *Feldzüge,* III, 555.

presence of Saint Germain and his *réserve,* but in spite of it.[54]
When Soubise was given the marshal's baton for the victory
at Lütterberg, his enemies insisted that the battle had been
won for him by his subordinate, Chevert.[55] An anonymous
wit defended the elevation of Soubise on the grounds that it
was the blind man who needed a *batôn,* not the man who led
him around.[56]

General officers frequently expressed contempt for their
superiors. On the eve of Minden, Broglie remarked to his as-
sociates that Contades's battle plan was "worthless." [57] When
an officer asked Saint Germain to point out the position of
the enemy, the caustic general turned his field glass on Clermont's headquarters and said: "The enemy is there." [58]

In 1759 Marshal Broglie formulated what he considered
to be the minimal and indispensable prerogatives of a field
commander:

> I would want, then, to be the master of the choice of my
> staff and general officers; to be sure of the means necessary
> for the execution of projects assigned to me; to have in my
> portfolio, in blank, rewards for each grade; to likewise be
> able to punish those who fail; and to have a direct corre-
> spondence with my master, to be sure that he received the
> truth, and that I received his wishes in all their clarity,
> unobscured by any commentary.[59]

These demands, which in truth are very modest, were never
accorded by the government of Louis XV. What the court
preferred were pliable and subservient instruments eager to
conform to every impulse from Versailles. This was particularly true during the administrations of Belle-Isle and

54. Mercoyrol de Beaulieu, *Campagnes,* p. 214.
55. Barbier, *Journal,* VII, 100; Duclos, *Mémoires,* II, 304.
56. This poem is found in A² 34–108.
57. Captured letter of a French officer, dated Aug. 4, 1759, in
Westphalen, *Feldzüge,* III, 550.
58. *Correspondance Saint Germain–Paris Duverney,* prefatory "Vie de
Saint Germain," I, 15–16; Mouffle d'Angerville, *Louis XV,* II, 131.
59. Broglie's letter to his uncle, Abbé de Broglie, Aug. 1759, quoted in
Broglie, *Secret,* I, 352.

Choiseul, both strong-willed men with military backgrounds. It is significant that the careers of Broglie and Saint Germain —the two generals with the most talent, initiative, and independence of spirit—ended in disaster. At the end of the war they were both in disgrace and in exile. In contrast the lackluster Soubise tranquilly pursued his career year after year in spite of his defeats and in the face of great public outcry against his incompetence.[60]

The court often showed a marked predilection for a system which divided the functions of command. A compliant general was given the title, but a reliable mentor directed his activities. General Mortaigne, a personal friend of Belle-Isle, served in this capacity under the unwilling Clermont.[61] In a like manner D'Estrées was sent to "concert" with Contades after Minden.[62] In 1760 the court tried unsuccessfully to interest Broglie and Saint Germain in serving as tutor to the young and inexperienced Prince of Condé.[63]

The French concept of command, distorted and frustrated as it was, proved a terrible handicap, and its failings are obvious when compared with the system used by France's enemies. In the case of Frederick, supreme authority and field command were both concentrated in the hands of the Warrior-King, seconded by a group of subordinates of

60. The over-all quality of French generalship has been assessed by the eminent military historian Delbrück: "Die Hofgenerale des Spanischen Erbfolge-krieges und des Siebenjährigen Krieges, die mit Frau von Maintenon und Frau von Pompadour über ihre kriegspläne correspondieren und fortwährend gegen einander intrigieren, ermangeln der grosser kriegerischen Entschlossenheit, die zuletzt in der Heerführung die entscheidende Eigenschaften ist. An persönlich Tapferkeit und an Eifer fehlt es ihnen nicht, wohl aber an der eigentlich kriegerischen, den ganzen Mann einnehmenden Gesinnung." Hans Delbrück, *Geschichte der Kriegskunst im Rahmen der politischen Geschichte* (Berlin, 1900–1920), IV, 301–2.
61. Speaking of his defeat at Krefeldt, Clermont remarked that Belle-Isle had wasted his time in sending him a tutor, for he could have done as well by himself. Jean-Baptiste-Donatien de Vimeur, comte de Rochambeau, *Mémoires militaires, historiques et politiques* (Paris, 1809), I, 116; Mercoyrol de Beaulieu, *Campagnes*, p. 187.
62. See the very revealing intercepted letter of D'Estrées dated Aug. 28, 1759, in Westphalen, *Feldzüge*, III, 748.
63. Broglie, *Secret*, I, 346; Mention, *Saint Germain*, Introduction, p. xix.

proven merit. Ferdinand of Brunswick held a difficult command because he was serving two masters—Frederick and George II. Ferdinand's correspondence reveals that he had all the difficulties that might be expected with an army composed of the contingents of six nations and dependent for its supply and finance upon credits voted by the English Parliament. In the actual conduct of operations, however, Ferdinand had much greater latitude than his French counterparts. The many letters he received from Frederick were filled with suggestions and advice, but the spirit of the interchange was one of amicable co-operation.[64] With all his pretentions to military prowess, George II had the good sense to confide in Ferdinand's abilities; in his occasional letters the monarch limited himself to expressions of approval and confidence.[65]

64. All of Frederick's correspondence with Ferdinand is reproduced in Westphalen's *Feldzüge.*

65. "Also ist Mein Zutrauen zu Eu. Lbd. Prudenz und Capacité so gross, dass Ich ohne einiges Bedenken es zu Deroselben Ermässigung und Entscheidung verstelle." George II to Ferdinand, July 2, 1759, *ibid.,* III, 325.

3

The Field Army

The nation's hopes for victory lay in the successful operation of the field armies, those huge and complex machines whose maintenance absorbed the great bulk of the war effort. The field army did not exist during time of peace; at the opening of hostilities it was put together by brigading pre-existing or hastily created regiments. The court gave the army a name, selected a commander and an intendant, and provided a plan of campaign. At the same time it posted officers for staff duty and made arrangements for the army's logistical needs.

Once called into being, the field army always maintained something of a tentative existence; it underwent frequent transformations dictated by circumstances or by the whims of Versailles. Each subsequent campaign saw a new plan and usually a new commander. The force might be increased or reduced at the expense of another army, or it might lose its identity through a merger with another command. At the conclusion of the war the entire mechanism was dismantled, and the constituent regiments dissolved or returned to provincial garrisons.

As a result of this practice the military establishment possessed no permanent staff organization and indeed no permanent unit larger than the regiment. The regiments were, as an officer nostalgically wrote, "a society, a family, where resided friendship, bravery, and honor." [1] The component battalions or squadrons were the basic combat and training units.

The constituent elements of the army display a confusing

1. Ray, *Réflexions*, p. 14.

proliferation of variations. Most mounted corps were composed of two squadrons; *Colonel-Général,* however, had three, and the *Carabiniers* had ten. The *Gendarmerie* had no squadron structure at all.[2] In January, 1762, there were twelve infantry regiments with four battalions, one with three battalions, fifty-two with two battalions, and nineteen with one battalion.[3] Battalions and squadrons varied in the number and strength of their companies. Infantry companies ranged in size from forty to eighty men.[4] The strength of mounted companies varied from thirty to seventy-five.[5] Added to this confusing picture were the *maison du roi* or household troops, the militia, and the foreign regiments in French service, all with their distinctive structures.[6] For present purposes it is perhaps best to note the disparity and indicate the composition of the majority of infantry and cavalry regiments (Table 1).

The third component, the artillery, had only recently been militarized and was still regarded as a "useful accessory," rather than an arm of the service.[7] From 1755 to 1758 the artillery was combined with the engineers to form the *Corps Royal d'Artillerie et de Génie.*[8] By eighteenth-century standards the French armies were well supplied with artillery.[9]

2. Maurice Sautai and Edmond Desbrière, *La cavalerie de 1740 à 1789* (Paris, 1904), p. 13; Dussauge, *Etudes,* p. 168.
3. Capitaine d'infanterie Bacquet, *L'infanterie au XVIIIe siècle; l'organisation* (Paris, 1907), p. 52.
4. *Ibid.,* n. 1.
5. Dussauge, *Etudes,* pp. 171, 173.
6. Details of regimental organization can be found in the authoritative work of Lucien Mouillard, *Les régiments sous Louis XV. Constitution de tous les corps de troupe pendant les Guerres de Succession à l'Empire et de Sept Ans* (Paris, 1882).
7. Jacques-Antoine-Hippolyte de Guibert, *Essai général de tactique* (*Œuvres militaires* [Paris, 1803]), I, 445.
8. The combination of the two services was the work of the eminent artillerist Vallière. The arrangement was not a satisfactory one, and Belle-Isle separated the two functions in 1758. Louis Mention, *L'armée de l'ancien régime de Louis XIV à la Révolution* (Paris, n.d.), p. 206.
9. Indeed Guibert considered the armies oversupplied. See his *Tactique,* I, 466.

Clermont's army had eighty field pieces, and large detachments of cannoniers, sappers, and workers.[10]

These three arms, with the addition of light troops, constituted the combat element of the field force. Something must now be said of the arrangement of these corps, particularly in the order of battle. While the complex subject of eighteenth-century tactics lies outside the scope of the present work, some brief explanations will be of great service in understanding administrative problems.[11]

During the active or campaign months the army was usually in one of three attitudes: encamped, in columns of march, or in order of battle. The last of these was of critical importance, since it was in this formation that the army engaged the enemy. There were two parallel battle lines, the center of each being composed of infantry, flanked by wings of cavalry. The two battle lines thus composed six divisions, to which was added a seventh, the *réserve*. In the *réserve* were placed special troops for shock or support purposes. Nominally the artillery was placed here also, since its use in the battle lines varied with circumstances. The army fought in linear formation, the so-called *ordre mince*. The *ordonnances* prescribed two ranks for the cavalry and three for the infantry.[12] Subsequently reference will be made to the order of battle, and for purposes of illustration one such formation has been reproduced in Table 3.

The combat elements of the field force fell most directly under the supervision of the commander. The chief administrative agency in this connection was the *état-major de*

---

10. "Ordre de Bataille de l'Armée aux ordres de S.A.S. M. le Comte de Clermont," June 17, 1758, A¹ 3477–119.

11. The literature on eighteenth-century tactics is exceedingly rich. To the classical treatises of Guibert, Frederick, and Jomini may be added many other critical studies by later generations. A valuable introduction to the whole subject is provided by Robert S. Quimby, *The Background to Napoleonic Warfare: The Theory of Military Tactics in Eighteenth Century France* (New York, 1957).

12. Sautai and Desbrière, *Cavalerie*, p. 21; Mention, *Saint Germain*, p. 194.

l'armée, or army staff, whose chief bore the title of *maréchal général des logis de l'armée,* and was assisted by numerous *aides-maréchaux.* Administrative directives were passed to the staffs of infantry and cavalry for transmission to the majors, the regimental officers charged with the details of administration. (See Table 2.) The *maréchal général* had no authority over the troops, and such orders as he issued came from the general commanding.[13] In addition the *maréchal général* and his subordinates performed a wide variety of functions touching the army's movement, intelligence, and distribution of supplies. The range of activities is well illustrated by the "departments" into which Broglie organized his staff in 1760:

> *First Department* (M. de Chaulieu): opening of marches, reconnaissance of camps.
> *Second Department* (M. de Baudouin): reconnaissance of terrain, direction of the *ingénieurs-géographes* (cartographers).
> *Third Department* (M. de Dommangeville and M. de Montaut): green and dry forage, wood and straw for soldiers' fires and beds.
> *Fourth Department* (Baron de Bon): secret correspondence, direction of two companies of guides, fusiliers, and peasants.
> *Fifth Department* (M. Dennery): daily correspondence with infantry and cavalry staffs, commander of artillery, intendant, *régisseurs* and entrepreneurs.
> *Sixth Department* (Chev. de Villefranches): direction of *fourriers* (quartering officers), wagonmasters, baggage, forage for headquarters.[14]

Despite the great importance of the *état-major,* it was not a truly technical organ staffed with specialists. Since there was no permanent staff organization in the military establishment, the service had to be thrown together at the beginning

---

13. Léon Hennet, *Regards en arrière. Etudes d'histoire militaire sur le XVIII⁰ siècle. L'Etat-major* (Paris, 1911), p. 146.
14. "Départmens de Mrs. les Aydes Maréchaux des Logis de l'Armée," June 15, 1760, A² 44–12.

of hostilities by drawing on the cadres of line officers. Staff service was highly coveted, and appointments were usually awarded to influence rather than to specialized knowledge. Even the official attitude reflected the disdain for "technicians." The *ordonnance* of March 10, 1759, expressly prohibited officers of the corps of engineers from serving on the *état-major*.[15] It is not surprising, then, that the staff gave evidence of "too much pride and too little knowledge." [16]

The logistical functions of the *maréchal général* required close co-operation with another functionary, the intendant. To the intendant was confided a vast area of administration usually referred to as the *service*—supply, subsistence, finance, military police, transport, and hospital service.[17] It was the intendant who brought the army into existence, supervising the marshaling of its elements; [18] the commander arrived only after the army was formed and ready for operations. In the field his role was second only to that of the commander, and he was aided by a score or so of *commissaires des guerres*.[19] Much of his work was done in close co-operation with the *état-major*—the planning of marches, distribution of supplies, verifying of regimental rolls, etc. He had supervision of the system of requisition used

---

15. Mention, *Saint Germain*, pp. 184–85.

16. General Mortaigne to Belle-Isle, July 20, 1758, A¹ 3479–106.

17. For an excellent description of the functions of the intendant, see D. Molias *et al.*, "Le corps de l'intendance militaire," *Revue historique de l'armée*, XIII, No. 4 (1957), 83–124.

18. The role of the intendant in the formation of the army of Soubise in 1757 is described in detail in Lieutenant Charles-Nicolas Dublanchy, *Une intendance d'armée au XVIIIᵉ siècle. Etude sur les services administratifs à l'armée de Soubise pendant la Guerre de Sept Ans, d'après la correspondance et les papiers inédits de l'intendant François-Marie Gayot* (Paris, 1908), pp. 30–40.

19. All of these posts were extremely well paid and conferred nobility. Gayot received 1,000 livres per month along with fifty rations of bread and thirty of forage. The *commissaires* received from 250 to 800 livres per month and similarly generous rations of bread and forage. "Tableau du traitement attribu aux officiers généraux de tous grades à commencer du Pce. du Sang commandant en chef et autres employés dans une armée, tant par mois de trente jours que par mois de quarante-cinq jours" (no date), A² 35–36.

in occupied territories, and he negotiated contracts for the army's needs. In addition he was the chief fiscal officer. One of the intendant's functions was the supervision of the various public and private corporations which supplied very diverse services—the bread company or *munitionnaire,* the meat supplier, the forage *régie,*[20] the entrepreneurs for the hospitals, and so on. These organizations will be examined in detail elsewhere, and it will suffice here to note their importance as parts of the field force.

The intendant bore a royal commission, and though he was nominally subordinate to the commander, he had the right of direct correspondence with Versailles. His opinion carried much weight in the conduct of the campaign, and he could in fact exercise a veto over proposed campaigns.

Since the welfare of the army depended to a large degree upon the intendant, his close co-operation with the commander was indispensable for a successful campaign, but in practice this co-operation was all too often marred by bitter quarrels. The conflicts arose in part from the rather vague nature of the intendant's competence. His duties were not delineated in any *ordonnance,* and his relationship to the commander was highly colored by personal consideration.[21] The intendant was a civil functionary drawn from the *noblesse de robe,* and these qualities did not endear him to the military. Since the intendants were all clients of Paris Duverney they were not immune to court intrigues.

20. The *régie* was a government concern that had many of the characteristics of a private company, its own budget, employees, equipment, etc.

21. Understandably Paris Duverney accorded to the intendant the widest possible latitude, and lectured Clermont on the dangers of meddling in the intendant's domain: "Il est, monseigneur, deux espèces d'administrations dans une armée, l'une militaire, l'autre civile. Si le général qui est placé à la tête des deux . . . souffre que l'épée prenne une supériorité despotique sur la plume . . . il serait bien difficile qu'il parvient à mettre entre toutes les parties qui composent son armée, l'harmonie et l'ensemble qui peuvent seuls en assurer les opérations." Paris Duverney to Clermont, May 16, 1758, Gayot Manuscripts, Bibliothéque de Nancy, Vol. 643, MS 104. The Gayot MSS will henceforth be cited simply by volume and manuscript number, e.g. 643–104.

François-Marie Gayot, intendant of the Army of the Lower Rhine from 1757 to 1759, was one of the most able of these functionaries, and his correspondence reveals him as a moderate and conscientious servant; yet his career was marred by constant difficulties with his superiors. When he was first posted to the army, Richelieu suspected him as an agent sent to foment trouble.[22] Clermont took a violent dislike to him and tried without success to get him recalled.[23] With Contades, by contrast, Gayot got on quite well. When Paris Duverney inquired about Gayot's relations with Broglie, Gayot's brother replied in terms which serve admirably to illustrate the disdain with which the military regarded the functions of the intendant:

> You embarrass me very much by asking me how my brother gets along with the Duc de Broglie. . . . Merit has little prerogative when the person displeases. I fear that my brother is in this case—without, however, being able to say so with surety; and I am inclined to think that the Duc de Broglie does not put tremendous store in what is called administration, nor consequently in those charged with it; thus nothing would surprise me.[24]

In the administrative structure of the field army we find the same differentiation of functions which existed at court. At Versailles the strategic and logistical considerations found their spokesmen in the minister and Duverney respectively. The same division is represented in the field by the "military" functions of the commander and the "civil" ones of the intendant. The evidence is overwhelming that in neither place did the system of "pulling in double harness" work smoothly.

The system of dual command—for it was very nearly that —was justified and perhaps dictated by circumstances. The field army had become an enormous and highly intricate mechanism; making it work efficiently with the primitive administrative methods of the times required a continual and

---

22. *Mémoire particulière* of Gayot, Gayot MSS, 644–285.
23. The controversy is recounted in Rousset, *Gisors*, pp. 429–441.
24. M. de Bellombre to Paris Duverney, Oct. 4, 1759, A² 60–21.

exhausting effort that taxed to the utmost the abilities of both commander and intendant. The purely "military" functions of command were difficult enough, considering for example, that an army of one hundred battalions and one hundred squadrons would present a battle line eight miles long.[25] The commander was already overburdened, as Guibert revealed so eloquently:

> He is absorbed in details, blinded by their immensity, dazed by their multiplicity; a hundred thousand men whose movements he must direct; all the obstacles produced by our bad constitution; a hundred thousand enemies who oppose him; a plan of campaign with several parts; arrangements without number resulting from the multiplicity of objectives; so many attentions combined form a burden beyond his forces. He is always fatigued and crushed under it, or at most he moves but feebly, and with only a part of his faculties.[26]

Military administration betrayed the same basic weakness that proved the undoing of the old regime—not so much a surfeit of authority but rather a lack of it. Neither the monarch nor his military leaders could wield the power that was theirs in theory. In both cases much was alienated to vested interests. As a result the purview of both commander and intendant was hedged by countless considerations, and vast areas lay beyond their effective control. A commander could count himself fortunate if his fellow officers accorded him anything more than the status of *primus inter pares*. Though he led the "King's Army," in a very real sense that army was not royal property, but the possession of proprietary colonels and captains who trained, equipped, and led their own men.[27] The intendant was similarly frustrated; though he

25. Guibert, *Défense du système de guerre moderne* (*Œuvres militaires*), III, 12–13.
26. Guibert, *Tactique*, I, 84.
27. The *maison du roi* or household troops escaped even the jurisdiction of the minister of war, their commanders recognizing no authority save that of the king. Similarly the commanders of the cavalry regiments *Mestre-de-Camp Général* and *Commissaire Général* thwarted the commanders, inspectors, and *ordonnances,* and ruled their regiments like petty sovereigns. Mention, *Saint Germain*, pp. 25, 83.

was responsible for the logistical services, he was often reduced to negotiating with the powerful concerns which supplied those services. In sum the military establishment was not yet completely "militarized" with clear, systematic, and convergent channels of responsibility.

This fault bred still another, which also is equally applicable to the regime in general. The rational and the logical have always been considered traits which peculiarly appeal to the French, and if there was any century in which the attraction was paramount it was the Age of Reason. But the army, like the state it served, found it exceedingly difficult to extricate itself from a labyrinth of privilege and tradition, and to achieve the efficiency that comes from rational and uniform procedures. In the army there was a strong conservative spirit, with a deep hostility toward change or reform. Some military customs indicate careful preservation for centuries. When a besieged garrison surrendered, the capitulation still contained the sixteenth-century formula by which the defenders were to march "out of the breach with flags unfurled, drums beating, and matches lit." [28] In the earlier centuries the artillery had the right to the bells in a successfully besieged town, the precious bell metal being used to cast cannon; in the eighteenth century the custom was still preserved, though commuted to a special tax, the *rachat des cloches*.[29]

Some regiments enjoyed special distinctions; the *Cuirassiers* cavalry regiment was the only one which still wore the full breastplate, in commemoration of its spirited crossing of the Rhine in 1672 under the eyes of Louis XIV.[30] Such customs were harmless enough, and even beneficial, in that they contributed to that elusive quality, *esprit de corps*.

The proliferation of these traditions was excessive; it robbed the army of uniformity and made the administrator's

28. Audouin, *Administration*, I, 287.
29. *Ibid.*, II, 136.
30. Dussauge, *Etudes*, p. 171.

work a nightmare. We have already noticed the illogical variation in the strength of regiments and even companies. The regiments also varied greatly in quality, the result of a longstanding caste system. The wealthier and more desirable infantry regiments were the oldest in order of creation—six *vieux* and six *petits vieux*.[31] An unbroken order of precedence stretched down to the most recently created and most ill-kept regiments. Even the pay of the common soldier varied from one regiment to another.[32] The simple drawing up of an order of battle presented all sorts of problems. By tradition the oldest regiments had to be given the *postes d'honneur,* the most exposed positions on the wings.[33] The Swiss regiments would not permit themselves to be brigaded with French units, the practice being "contrary to their privileges." [34] If a small contingent of horsemen were needed for reconnaissance or picket duty, the commander could not order a captain to risk the destruction of his company in such hazardous duty. A special troop had to be formed from all the companies of a regiment or brigade.[35] If orders of march were prepared, the oldest brigade took the head of the column.[36] The *Gendarmerie* had to be given a separate route for each of its sixteen companies.[37] Even in the order of march for the baggage train, precedence had to be observed in great detail; by custom the baggage of the *maréchal général des logi*s had to follow that of the *mestre-de-camp général* of the cavalry.[38] The dragoons had to be given their

31. The *Régiment du Roi* was probably the most "exclusive" of the line infantry regiments; the King was its colonel and inspector. *Ibid.,* p. 103.

32. *Fitzjames,* an Irish regiment, had the highest pay of the line regiments, being on a par with that of the British cavalry. *Ibid.,* p. 172.

33. Guillaume Le Blond, "Postes d'honneur," *Encyclopédie, ou dictionnaire raisonné des sciences, des arts et des métiers,* ed. Denis Diderot *et al.* (Paris, 1751–1765), XIII, 270.

34. Contades to Belle-Isle, May 1, 1759, A^1 3518–8.

35. Sautai and Desbrière, *Cavalerie,* p. 3.

36. *Ibid.,* p. 17.

37. Dussauge, *Etudes,* p. 262.

38. Hennet, *Etat-major,* p. 39. See also Paul-Jean-Michel-Raoul Frémont, *Les payeurs d'armées. Historique du service de la trésorerie et des postes aux armées, 1293–1870* (Paris, 1906), p. 50.

marching orders separately, since their commander refused to recognize the authority of the cavalry staff.[39]

The field army, then, was far from a homogeneous force; its elements were disparate and sometimes antagonistic. Those who led it and saw to its functioning were in the unenviable position of having responsibility without authority. To be sure, the machine worked, but by dint of herculean effort and with only a modicum of success. The disastrous experience of the Seven Years' War seemed to prove its senescence; and anguished officers like Guibert were hoping for some extraordinary authority who could consolidate the military establishment. "The machine is so worn out that even a man of genius could only touch it with trepidation. His genius would not suffice to guarantee his success. What is needed is no less than a king among ministers or a king who is minister." [40]

39. Mention, *Saint Germain,* p. 83.
40. Guibert, *Guerre moderne,* IV, 207.

4

Planning

Military historians are known for the proverbial accuracy and completeness with which they report each detail: the placing of a battery, the march of a battalion, the decision to lay siege to one town in preference to another—indeed, the smallest move on the vast chess board on which the game of war is played. What is not so well known is the staff work that precedes each move, however minor it might be. This often neglected procedure, that of planning, must now be examined.

At the highest level planning involves the war policies—the end purposes for which the nation fights and the strategic means which are selected to achieve those purposes. In the Seven Years' War this "grand strategy" immediately poses the question of France's relations with her allies, all of whom had bound themselves to co-operation in a joint effort. In fact the possibility of combined or closely co-ordinated operations was very limited; the failure of the several allies to act in close concert was one of the factors which enabled Frederick to survive in the middle of a sea of enemies.

The French government was largely responsible for the notable lack of co-operation, particularly with Austria. For France the chief enemy was England, and operations in the European theater were designed not so much to dismantle Prussia as to gain possession of Hanover, which would enable France to come to the peace table with her "hands full." [1] Moreover the legal position of the French in Germany was that of "auxiliaries" to Austria, as guarantors of the Peace of Westphalia. The consequences in operations were that in

1. Bernis to Clermont, May 12, 1758, A² 37–113.

any combination of French and Austrian armies the role of
the French would be secondary, and the commander would
be designated by Vienna. When one experiment of this kind
ended in the disaster at Rosbach, the French were very careful not to repeat the mistake. Indeed, the French in their
humiliation became bitterly critical of their traditional
enemy, now their most important ally. This attitude was fully
as widespread as the ill-concealed admiration for Frederick
II. General de Muy wrote indignantly to the minister lament-
ing the "too scrupulous fidelity" which produced Rosbach.[2]
Another general felt that it smacked of treason against the
interests of France.[3]

The attitude in governmental circles was similar, and
found official expression in a letter of Choiseul:

> For the past two years the King's ministry has occupied it-
> self with separating as far as possible its military operations
> from those of His Majesty's allies. There are two purposes
> in this separation. The first is not to derange the plans of the
> King's allies if circumstances should become favorable for a
> separate peace with England. The second is not to run the
> risk of subordinating a part of our troops and means to the
> will of the King's allies, it being certain that we can draw no
> advantage from this.[4]

Each winter overtures came from Vienna in view to a
co-ordinated plan of operations, and on each occasion the
French government rejected the proposals politely but
firmly. In January, 1759, the Austrian government submitted

2. Muy to Belle-Isle, June 8, 1759, A[1] 3517–105.
3. Bourcet, *Mémoires,* I, 3–4. It should be added that any merger of
Austrian and French forces produced a host of delicate questions of
etiquette and precedence, matters of no little concern in the eighteenth
century. An attempt was made to settle these questions by negotiation
between the two courts. See the *Convention entre le Roi Très Chrétien et
l'Impératrice Reine de Hongrie et de Bohème, sur le service de leurs armées
combinées du 25 février 1757* (Imprimerie royale, 1757). This published
accord and the *ordonnances* which will subsequently be cited are from the
collection *Ordonnances militaires,* preserved in the Archives de la Guerre
under the catalog number H34.
4. Choiseul to Broglie, Aug. 21, 1760, A[1] 3559–71.

a highly detailed project for a concentration of French, Austrian, and Russian armies to bring Frederick to bay between the Oder and the Elbe.[5] Versailles replied that the concentration of forces would create a tremendous supply problem, and suggested that "each of the allied powers should prepare its own attack." [6] A month later the Austrian court knew it was fighting a losing battle in getting its grand strategy adopted, and it deferred to the French view, albeit with a note of displeasure. "All that can be said is that it is very regrettable that it [the Austrian plan] cannot be effected." [7]

The disinclination of the French toward any close co-operation is reflected in the relations of French and Austrian commanders whose armies operated in the same theater. When the Austrian commander in Franconia, the Prince of Deux Ponts, asked Broglie for a diversion to relieve the pressure on his army, Broglie responded with a multitude of reasons why he could not oblige, and expressed the belief that Deux Ponts's "prudence, ability, and vigilance" would suffice to extricate him from the dilemma.[8] The ministry fully approved Broglie's refusal to help, and the argument it advanced is revealing: "It is up to the army of the Empire to fulfil this obligation. . . . Whatever the case, it is not for us directly to aid this part of the Empire." [9]

Having thus largely divorced themselves from the projects of the other allies, the French planned their own campaigns after going through the formality of "consultations." Even so

5. "Mémoire ou projet de campagne proposé par la cour de Vienne, janvier, 1759," A¹ 3511–1.

6. "Mémoire, janvier, 1759," A¹ 3511–2. Whatever its motive, the French government was justified in raising the question of supply. Bourcet, who was an authority second to none, stated in his memoirs that such a union as the Austrians proposed was logistically impossible, there being no place in Germany where such a force could subsist. *Mémoires,* I, 10.

7. "Mémoire, février, 1759," A¹ 3512–72.

8. Broglie to Deux Ponts, May 12, 1759, A¹ 3515–124.

9. Belle-Isle to Contades, May 13, 1759, A¹ 3515–132. The two allies did agree to break off operations and enter winter quarters simultaneously, so that Frederick and Ferdinand would have no opportunity to shift their effectives back and forth. Belle-Isle to Contades, September 12, 1759, A¹ 3522–200.

the task was a difficult one, owing to the multitude of factors that had to be taken into account. When Crémilles was asked to submit proposals for operations in 1758, he drew up a long list of questions on which he asked instructions before beginning:

1. What will be the disposition of Prussian forces and matériel?
2. What is the possibility of Danish and Dutch belligerence?
3. What will the Hanoverian strength be, and what the possibility of English aid?
4. What will be the disposition of the forces of the Empress?
5. Can the Russians be depended upon?
6. Will Brunswick and Hesse join the allies or continue to side with the enemy?
7. Will the two allies operate jointly?
8. Will a corps be detached from the Army of the Lower Rhine?
9. What can be expected of the Swedish Army?
10. What use will be made of the Army of the Empire? [10]

It was in cabinet discussions that answers were sought to these questions. The discussions took place in the winter months and the field commanders returned to take part in the deliberations.[11] Here the projects prepared by the army staffs were examined and a final decision made. The final plan was always the same—to push Ferdinand back and occupy Hanover and the Prussian dependencies throughout the winter. Within this framework an attempt was made to foresee the possible reactions of the enemy and to counteract them, and also to take measures against any initiative on Ferdinand's part, particularly the possibility that he would attempt a winter campaign. The size and dispositions of the French forces were agreed upon. Lines of advance were planned based on staff and intelligence reports on the avail-

10. "Mémoire, 30 janvier 1758," A¹ 3471–201.
11. Thus D'Estrées and Soubise took part in the formulation of the campaign of 1757. Luçay, *Secrétaires d'état*, p. 93.

ability of forage and other provisions in the proposed area of operations. At the same time the path of advance was drawn so as to utilize to the maximum the river system for supply lines. Finally the date for the beginning of operations was set—usually in the months of June or July, when green forage would be sufficiently plentiful to ease the subsistence problem.[12]

Fully as much attention was given to the planning of winter quarters. Indeed one of the chief goals of the campaign was to place the troops in areas suitable for this purpose by November, when the armies usually suspended operations. If at all possible the troops were quartered on enemy territory, since their needs could be exacted from the population, and much money saved.[13] The inactive period was absolutely necessary to repair an army after a hard and wearing campaign; so the winter quarters had to be secure from enemy incursion. To this end the emplacements were usually arranged in four parallel lines with a cordon of light troops in front of the first line.[14] The garrisons were to be sufficiently close together so as to be assembled into sizable units within forty-eight hours.[15] Further to insure the tranquility of winter quarters the region in front of them was laid waste in order to hamper the enemy's advance.[16]

12. See, for example, "Résultat de la conférence tenue chez M. le Maal. de Belle-Isle le 18 février 1759 sur les opérations de la campagne prochaine en Allemagne," A¹ 3512–74.
13. "Vous n'ignorez pas l'épuisement de nos finances. Elles ne suffiront jamais s'il faut que toutes les troupes du Roy hivernent dans les pays qui appartiennent à nos alliés ou à des princes neutres (où il faudra tout payer du Trésor royal). A l'exception du Duché de Clèves, objet extrèmement médiocre, tout ce qui est en deça du Rhin se trouve dans ce dernier cas. Il serait donc de la dernière importance et en quelque manière nécessaire que nous puissions occuper la Hesse pendant l'hiver." Belle-Isle to Contades, Aug. 17, 1758, A¹ 3481–33.
14. "Etat G^{al} des Quartiers de l'Armée du Bas Rhin, 12 novembre 1758," A¹ 3486–214.
15. Mercoyrol de Beaulieu, *Campagnes*, p. 210.
16. See in this connection Belle-Isle's instructions to Contades of Oct. 16, 1758, A¹ 3485–3.

The project for winter quarters was drawn up by the *maréchal général* in consultation with the commanding general; the proposal was then submitted to the intendant for his criticisms and then forwarded to Versailles. It was often difficult to satisfy military, political, and logistical requirements, and from August to October of 1758 no fewer than four plans were submitted.[17] The final plan, embodying the thoughts of the ministry and the intendant, was not completed until November 12.[18]

In fulfilling the objectives set by the court, the field commander exercised considerable tactical latitude, and the everyday activities of the army could only be followed by an anxious court. Therefore operational planning on the day-to-day or tactical level was largely done through the army's staff. The information supplied through the staff and its adjuncts was of extreme value in helping the commander reach his decisions. If, for example, a march in a particular direction were contemplated, the *ingénieurs-géographes* were called upon to provide accurate maps; reconnaissance would supply the *maréchal général* with the approximate location of the enemy and the condition of the roads. Once the move was decided upon the commander's intentions were then transmitted to the wagonmasters who directed the baggage trains and the quartering officers who laid out the camp at the end of the march. The intendant was also informed, and he in turn took the necessary logistical measures, insuring that the *munitionnaire* would be able to deliver bread, and that supplies would also be available from the other services. Often these logistical considerations forced the commander to alter his original plan, usually on the representations of the

17. See "Mémoire ou projet de Quartiers d'Hiver pour l'Armée du Bas Rhin, 29 août 1758," A¹ 3481–183; "Projet de Quartiers derrière le Rhin de 1758–1759, 3 septembre 1758" (with Gayot's annotations), A¹ 3482–42; "Nouveau Projet de Quartiers, 10 septembre 1758," A¹ 3482–179; "Quatrième Projet de Quartiers, 29 octobre 1758," A¹ 3485–243.
18. "Etat Gᵃˡ des Quartiers de l'Armée du Bas Rhin, 12 novembre 1758," A¹ 3486–214.

intendant.[19] When the army was operating in the territories of allied or neutral rulers, there were apt to be further complications. Since these rulers were to supply certain of the needs of the troops in transit, they insisted on being informed of proposed movements so that necessary preparations could be made to collect wood, straw, etc. Moreover they were prone to protesting to Versailles if they felt that they were unduly imposed upon. Many, like the Count of Neuwied, complained that their lands were "submerged with troops." [20] In some cases the intransigence of the local authorities could be overcome only through the offices of the French diplomatic representatives, who took up tedious negotiations which sometimes resolved the problem. On other occasions not even diplomatic overtures could overcome the resistance of the German authorities. The magistrate of Frankfort stubbornly refused to permit the French to move a powder train through the town since he considered it too dangerous. There was no choice but to go many miles out of the way to find another bridge over the Mein.[21]

These then were the mechanics and the problems of military planning, as they can be gleaned from the official records. Unfortunately little reference was made to these matters, but what remains testifies to the arduousness and complexities of planning, and to the many hours of staff work necessary before a single soldier was moved. The brief outline presented here will serve as an introduction to the subject, and as a frame of reference for the special problem of logistics, which will be treated in Chapter IX.

19. Thus when Clermont wanted to move a sizable cavalry force in the summer of 1758, Gayot insisted that it be divided into two separate forces with different itineraries, there being insufficient forage to move the entire force by the same route. Gayot's memoir of 1 June 1758, Gayot MSS, 645–145.

20. Comte de Neuwied to Belle-Isle, Nov. 29, 1758, A¹ 3508–279.

21. "Copie de la lettre que le magistrat de Francfort a écrit au ministre du Roy à Mayence le 29 mars 1758," A¹ 3508–159.

5

Intelligence

The task of collecting and evaluating data concerning the enemy—the function of military intelligence—is one of the little explored byways in the history of warfare; the importance of this staff function in the eighteenth century and the obscurity which has surrounded it warrant a careful examination.[1] Two centuries ago there was no formal military intelligence organization, and there was no counterpart to the specialist of the present day, the intelligence officer. The extreme value of accurate data concerning the enemy and his strength and movements was recognized during the Seven Years' War, and the French expended considerable time and money for this purpose. The random references scattered throughout the official records can provide a sketch of the French system of intelligence and also some evidence regarding its shortcomings.

In very primitive form there existed two levels or networks of military intelligence. The court was the nucleus for the first of these; it served as a clearing house for the information gathered by French diplomatic representatives and military observers attached to the armies of France's allies. These dispatches were usually routed to the ministry of war. Understandably the contents of these reports dealt mostly with the size and quality of *allied* forces, their movements, and the

---

1. Some information regarding military intelligence during the War of the Austrian Succession can be found in Colin, *Saxe*, I, 247–321. There is no study for the Seven Years' War; E. de Ribaucourt, *La vie et les exploits de J.-C. Fischer, brigadier des armées du Roy Louis XV, fondateur et commandant le corps des chasseurs (1743–1761), chef du service des renseignements* (Paris, 1929), is of very little value despite its promising title.

intentions of their leaders and their governments; judging from their instructions, these agents were to consider this as their "principal function." [2] Whatever information these representatives relayed concerning the enemy was usually limited to general estimates of strength and campaign plans; they seldom reported on the enemy's day to day movements, either because the data was not available, or more likely because it would have lost its value in the time lapse of communication.

The second network was that which would today be called field intelligence. It was directed by the field commander and processed by his staff when the army was assembled; when the army was dispersed in winter quarters and the commanding general absent, the work was carried on by various garrison commanders. This system was of permanent importance in the actual conduct of operations, and merits examination in detail.

Information concerning the enemy was obtained through several sources. Some of the military observers and diplomatic agents were sufficiently close to the area of operations to relay valuable tactical information, and were authorized to correspond directly with the field commander. The diplomatic agents in nearby posts were particularly useful in this regard, especially M. d'Affry at the Hague and M. Champeaux *père,* accredited to the Duke of Mecklenburg.[3] Firsthand information was sought by questioning deserters from the enemy and reconnaissances. The first of these sources figures very little in the official correspondence, but the second was relied upon heavily. Finally, each field commander had a special fund for

2. Letter of instructions of May 19, 1759, for the Marquis de Montalembert, Marc-René Montalembert, *Correspondance de M. le marquis de Montalembert, étant employé par le roi de France à l'armée suédoise, avec M. le marquis d'Havrincour, M. le maréchal de Richelieu, les ministres du Roi à Versailles, MM. les généraux suédois et autres, etc., pendant les campagnes de 1757, 58, 59, 60 et 61, pour servir à l'histoire de la dernière guerre* (London, 1777), II, 21.

3. M. Champeaux claimed to have secret correspondents in Berlin and in Ferdinand's army. See Champeaux to Belle-Isle, July 27, 1759, A¹ 3519–168.

"secret and unforeseen expenses," which was used for the maintenance of spies in the enemy's army and behind his lines.

These were the standard sources of information, but sometimes others were utilized. On occasion the French were able to intercept enemy correspondence, but this was uncommon. The chivalrous amenities which still governed the relations between opposing generals occasionally served as pretexts for espionage. Contades sent a *trompette* or herald to Ferdinand in the summer of 1759 in the secret hope of locating his position. The emissary was blindfolded as soon as he entered the enemy's lines, much to the chagrin of Contades.[4]

A comparison of French records with those of Ferdinand's army presents the clear impression that Ferdinand was consistently better informed. The advantage was telling; French officers frequently lamented Ferdinand's superiority in this regard: "He was informed of what happened in our camps, while our chiefs were not at all informed about what was happening in his." [5] These criticisms are borne out when French field intelligence is examined in detail and compared with the system of Ferdinand.

The information supplied by the French diplomatic agents, especially MM. Champeaux *père* and D'Affry, is much less detailed and seldom as accurate as the work of Ferdinand's agents. M. Haenichen, attached to the Brunswick legation at the Hague, was a priceless asset to the allied cause. His letters to Ferdinand's secretary reveal that he had numerous correspondents in Paris, from whom he received regular reports. Haenichen frequently enclosed intercepted letters from French commanders; he seems to have obtained copies of nearly all

4. Contades to Belle-Isle, June 22, 1759, A¹ 3517–283. Ferdinand was not above making similar efforts. He asked for permission for two of his officers to go to the baths at Geismar; Contades refused in the belief that the officers would be "two honest spies." Contades to Belle-Isle, June 17, 1759, A¹ 3517–221.

5. Mercoyrol de Beaulieu, *Campagnes*, p. 346. See also Rochambeau, *Mémoires*, I, 120; Ray, *Réflexions*, p. 166.

the confidential letters of M. Rouillé, who for a time was Louis' Minister of Foreign Affairs.[6]

The French were consistently at a disadvantage in the *petite guerre* or reconnaissance and patrol missions. The cavalry and dragoons, originally charged with this function, now considered it beneath their dignity; their former *élan* had been replaced by "slowness and formalism." [7] The hussars still fulfilled their role as a reconnaissance and patrol force, but their quality had much deteriorated. Maria Theresa could spare no Hungarians, the customary recruits for this branch, and the ranks were filled with a motley group of deserters and foreigners.[8] The service was held in low repute, and justifiably so. In 1758 an entire regiment was dissolved because of pillage and brigandage.[9] The light irregular troops were chiefly charged with reconnaissance. Though there were as many as ten thousand of these, they too were of inferior quality, particularly when pitted against Ferdinand's excellent light troops.[10] The French units seem to have been badly mounted.[11] Leadership was not of the best; the German Brigadier Fischer, their chief, was a protégé of Belle-Isle. Fischer was the subject of much complaint, and it is probable that he was not the paragon of military virtue portrayed by his admiring biographer.[12]

The efforts of the French to obtain the services of paid

6. Most of Haenichen's letters and enclosures are reproduced in Westphalen, *Feldzüge.*

7. Sautai and Desbrière, *Cavalerie,* p. 21.

8. Dussauge, *Etudes,* p. 173.

9. Barbier, *Journal,* VII, 52.

10. Westphalen, *Feldzüge,* IV, 101. The enemy regarded the French light troops as "n'étant nullement des gens à faire peur." Westphalen to Haenichen, May 5, 1759, *Feldzüge,* III, 225.

11. General Mortaigne to Belle-Isle, April 8, 1758, A¹ 3490–20.

12. The biography referred to here is that of Ribaucourt, previously cited. Clermont regarded Fischer as a "liar." Clermont to Belle-Isle, April 18, 1758, A¹ 3474–154. The German had a disturbing habit of disappearing for days; on one occasion the Chevalier de Ray was sent to locate him and found him and his entire corps deep in the mountains, eating and drinking in the chateau of the Count of Stolberg. Ray, *Réflexions,* p. 122.

spies were singularly unsuccessful, though lavish sums were spent for this purpose.[13] The populations of the various German states seem to have been overwhelmingly sympathetic to Frederick and Ferdinand.[14] Characteristically this nascent nationalism puzzled the French, and they attributed the attitude of the indigenous populations to religious fanaticism.[15]

What few spies the French could recruit seem to have been individuals of very little ability. They provided information of only the most rudimentary sort: rough estimates of the quantities of troops they had seen and descriptions of their uniforms.[16] There were few of these *misérables,* and Clermont considered them useful only for a haphazard reconnaissance of the enemy.[17] There was room for suspicion that these agents sometimes never made the reconnaissances and invented information for their pay. One of them produced an affidavit from an innkeeper behind enemy lines as proof that

13. In the first eleven months of 1758 the Army of the Lower Rhine spent 480,000 livres for "dépenses secrètes et inopinées." "Etat de la situation du trésorier au premier décembre 1758 sur les dépenses extraordinaires courantes de l'armée, déduction faite des fonds qui lui ont été remis jusqu'au dit jour," Gayot MSS, 650–184. Ferdinand spent far less for this purpose, only 11,000 pounds or 264,000 livres in 1759. "Etat de la dépense de l'armée du Prince Ferdinand d'une année à l'autre depuis l'arrivée de Mr. Hunter, Intendant General, jusqu'au 24 décembre 1761," Westphalen, *Feldzüge,* V, 1114.

14. "Pour quelque somme que ce soit on ne trouverait pas en Hesse un espion, pendant que l'ennemi est informé de nos moindres mouvements." D'Estrées to Belle-Isle, Sept. 3, 1759, A¹ 3522–47. Even in Saxony, whose dynasty was closely allied to that of France, the population was so favorable to Frederick's cause that Soubise could find no spies there. Mention, *Saint Germain,* Introduction, p. vii. See also Mercoyrol de Beaulieu, *Campagnes,* p. 211, and Bourcet, *Mémoires,* I, 130.

15. "Je conviens que le Roi de Prusse a su exiter tous les ministres protestants en sa faveur, et qu'il est parvenu à faire naitre une espèce de fanatisme dans presque tout l'empire." Belle-Ise to Clermont, Jan. 19, 1758, A² 35–1.

16. See for example "Rapport d'un homme envoyé à Marpurg du 2 juillet (1758)," A¹ 3478–5; "Rapport du voyage de Schultz, 23 février 1758," A² 39–58. The descriptions of uniforms enabled the French to identify various enemy units; for this purpose the staff possessed color charts of the dress of each enemy regiment. One of these has been preserved: "Etat nouveau de l'Armée anglaise, ou de la Grande Bretagne, comme elle se trouve effectivement l'année 1759," A¹ 3514–6.

17. Clermont to Paulmy, Feb. 16, 1758, A² 35–75.

he had indeed fulfilled his mission.[18] To supplement the sketchy data supplied by these men, the French tried other methods. Sometimes valets were drafted into the hazardous profession of the spy.[19] Officers with a knowledge of German were sent into the nearby Netherlands to glean whatever information they could there.[20] Expatriate Frenchmen resident in Germany were called upon, particularly a wine merchant established in Munster.[21]

Ferdinand profited immensely from German hostility toward the French. In Hesse the French could not place a single soldier "without the peasants going off to inform the enemy of it." [22] The enemy also had much better success with professional spies. Belle-Isle estimated that the English minister at Cologne had no fewer than eight excellent informants in his pay, four of them in the French Army of the Lower Rhine.[23] An anonymous French officer, referred to only as "Z," supplied Ferdinand with information regularly, and even passed through the lines to deliver the French order of battle.[24] The mysterious "Z" was not the only secret defector. An officer with Soubise also sent information, as did Major de Hoym of Fischer's corps.[25] There must have been many other informants in the French armies who did their work diligently, even reporting the gossip of the servants in the French camp.[26]

French commanders had great difficulty in collating and appraising what data they received. As was sometimes the case, there was too much information—most of it contra-

18. "Rapport de Philipe Lanot" (no date), A¹ 3474–146.
19. The Count of Chabot used his servant in this capacity. See Chabot to Clermont, March 17, 1758, A² 40–24.
20. Belle-Isle to Contades, Dec. 17, 1758, A¹ 3489–11.
21 His activities are described in the letter of the Marquis d'Armentières to Belle-Isle, March 29, 1759, A¹ 3513–217.
22. Baron de Bonneval to Belle-Isle, July 16, 1759, A¹ 3519–16.
23. Belle-Isle to Contades, July 23, 1758, A¹ 3479–157.
24. Westphalen to Haenichen, June 19, 1759, Westphalen, *Feldzüge*, III, 285.
25. See Ferdinand's memoir of Oct. 11, 1758, *ibid.*, II, 494; Ferdinand to Frederick, Nov. 4, 1757, *ibid.*, p. 210.
26. Ferdinand to Frederick, Oct. 4, 1757, *ibid.*, p. 67.

dictory. The exasperated Contades wrote that the variation in reports was "insupportable." [27]

The system was so unorganized that it was seldom possible to corroborate a report. On March 2, 1759, a spy reported that the enemy was building ovens at Stadt Lohn—an exceedingly important piece of information if true, since it would indicate Ferdinand's projected line of march.[28] The French commander in the area, M. de Saint Pern, made strenuous efforts to have the report verified. Ten days later he was still not completely sure, but was inclined to think the information false.[29]

Estimates of enemy strength were widely divergent, with the field commander characteristically preferring the larger figures and the court insisting on the weakness of opposing forces. At Krefeldt Ferdinand had 30,000 men; [30] Clermont insisted, however, that the enemy strength was no less than 60,000.[31] In 1760 the court estimated enemy strength at 30,000 to 40,000; [32] Broglie held that Ferdinand had 70,000 men.[33]

Much blame can be placed at the door of the commander for his failure to maintain the most elementary security measures. Headquarters was poorly policed, despite ministerial injunctions.[34] The camp was "like a fair, where anyone could come and go without the least question being asked." [35] This was hardly an exaggeration; on one occasion a German civilian was arrested near headquarters, carrying a field glass and a plan of the French camp.[36] General officers were

27. Contades to Belle-Isle, May 6, 1759, A¹ 3515–60.
28. The unsigned report is found in A¹ 3513–15.
29. Saint Pern to D'Armentières, March 12, 1759, A¹ 3513–17.
30. "Etat wie stark die Armee an Officiers, Unterofficiers und Gemeinen den 23 Juni 1758 in die Bataille gegangen," Westphalen, *Feldzüge*, I, 603.
31. Clermont to Belle-Isle, July 2, 1758, A² 38–140.
32. Belle-Isle to Broglie, May 29, 1760, A¹ 3554–307.
33. Broglie to Belle-Isle, May 24, 1760, A¹ 3554–216.
34. See for example Belle-Isle's letter to Contades of July 23, 1758, A¹ 3479–157.
35. Belle-Isle to Contades, Aug. 4, 1758, A¹ 3480–45.
36. General Cornillon to Belle-Isle, Aug. 1, 1758, A¹ 3480–18 *bis*.

notoriously prone to "leaking" information of a confidential nature. On the day before Minden Contades called a council of war, and great numbers of officers and men gathered outside headquarters to await the results of the deliberations. When the conference broke up the participants announced publicly: "Go sharpen your knives: battle tomorrow if Prince Ferdinand waits for us." [37] Soon the news was broadcast throughout the army; at 2:30 A.M. two deserters from the *Picardie* Regiment brought Ferdinand the news of the impending attack.[38] Broglie, it is true, took great pains to conceal his actions, but it was so uncommon for a general to keep his intentions to himself that it was considered nothing short of a "miracle." [39]

The French deficiency in obtaining information and in shielding their movements from the enemy sometimes produced disastrous results. When Ferdinand crossed the Rhine in the summer of 1758 after two months of preparations, the French were caught completely by surprise, and their ignorance of Ferdinand's intentions was rightly considered inexcusable.[40] In 1762 the activities of spies had been concentrated in the hands of Fischer, who took no pains to prevent his informants from learning one another's identity. One of his agents defected and denounced all the others, and in one fell blow the French were deprived of all their sources of information. The defeat at Grebenstein can be largely attributed to this calamity.[41] Such glaring shortcomings were symptomatic of the general deficiency in field intelligence that plagued the French armies throughout the conflict.

37. Mercoyrol de Beaulieu, *Campagnes,* p. 222.

38. *Ibid.,* p. 227; Westphalen to Haenichen, Aug. 5, 1759, Westphalen, *Feldzüge,* III, 521.

39. Intercepted letter of an unidentified French officer dated 14 July 1760, in Westphalen, *Feldzüge,* IV, 342.

40. See Belle-Isle's indignant letter of General Mortaigne, July 3, 1758, A¹ 3478–75.

41. Audouin, *Administration,* III, 201; Ribeaucourt, *Fischer,* p. 297.

6

Personnel: The Corps of Officers

In eighteenth-century France the corps of officers was an element of paramount importance in the military establishment. Not only were the cadres extremely numerous, they contained many of the most imposing and powerful figures in the realm. These led in the military the aristocratic reaction characteristic of the century. It is no wonder, then, that an enormous amount of attention was given them. The official correspondence is full of references to the myriad problems this imposing body created—advancement, morale, discipline, incentive, etc.

A distinction was always made between *officiers généraux* and *officiers particuliers*. There were four grades of general officers: *maréchal de France, lieutenant général, maréchal-de-camp,* and *brigadier.* The first of these was an exceptional distinction reserved for purposes of command.[1] The *lieutenant général* was the highest post regularly conferred, and also compatible with field command.[2] The same was not true, however, of the *maréchal-de-camp,* whose position was always one of immediate subordination.[3] The *brigadier,* as his

1. In 1758 the marshal's baton was held by sixteen officers. *Almanach Royal de 1758,* p. 96. The *maréchalat* corresponded to the English captain-general and the *Feldmarschall* in the German system. See the article "Marshal of France" in the military dictionary appended to the second volume of Antoine de Pas, marquis de Feuquières, *Memoirs of the late Marquis de Feuquières, Lieutenant-General of the French Army* (London, 1737).
2. The rank was equated with that of lieutenant general in the English service and the German *Feldmarschall-Leutnant.* See the article "Lieutenant General," *ibid.; Convention entre le Roi Très Chrétien, et d'Impératrice Reine de Hongrie et de Bohème, sur le service de leurs armées combinées du 25 février 1757.*
3. The English and German equivalents were major general and *Generalmajor* respectively. See the article "Marshal de Camp" in Feuquières' *Memoirs;* and the *Convention* cited above.

title implies, was charged with the command of a brigade; unlike the other general officers, he was not empowered to command horse and foot indiscriminately, but only the arm for which his commission was issued.[4]

The charges of general officers were not venal, but were awarded by seniority—the *ordre du tableau*—or for exceptionally distinguished service.[5] The commission entitled its holder to the endowments and considerations of his rank, but before he was actually called to service he had to be issued a *lettre de service* which expired at the end of the campaign, and was usually renewed before the army left quarters the following spring.[6]

The *officiers particuliers* were divided into two categories, the *officiers supérieurs*—colonel, lieutenant colonel, major, and captain—and the *officiers subalternes*—lieutenant and *sous lieutenant* or *enseigne* (*cornette* in the cavalry). Colonelcies and captaincies were purchased with ministerial approval, and involved considerable sums. In the older infantry regiments, the *vieux* and *petits vieux,* colonelcies cost as much as 75,000 livres.[7] Cavalry regiments were generally more costly; the Chevalier de Ray paid 100,000 livres for the colonelcy of the *Cuirassiers* regiment in 1762.[8] There was much variation in the price of companies, and in the more exclusive regiments a company was a large investment. Baron de Castelnau paid 7,000 livres for the *Carabiniers* company in 1760.[9] While the other regimental officers did not purchase their

4. The post was more a function than a rank, and was held concurrently by colonels, lieutenant colonels, and even captains. When the brigade was formed the officer holding the oldest commission as brigadier assumed the post. Hence a lieutenant colonel could command his own colonel. Sautai and Desbrière, *Cavalerie,* p. 13; Dussauge, *Etudes,* p. 284.

5. In 1759 the charges of *commissaire général* and *mestre-de-camp général* were sold for 266,000 livres and 332,000 livres respectively, the livre then being roughly equivalent to the English shilling. Belle-Isle to Madame de Castries, May 6, 1759, A¹ 3542–238. On the origin of these charges, see Luçay, *Secrétaires d'état,* pp. 489–98.

6. *Ibid.,* p. 488.

7. Bacquet, *Infanterie,* p. 18, n. 2.

8. Ray, *Réflexions,* p. 181.

9. Louis-Joseph-Amable de Richard, baron de Castelnau, *Lettres du baron de Castelnau, officier des carabiniers (1758–1793)* (Paris, 1911), p. 26.

commissions outright, they were nevertheless obliged to obtain the approval of both the ministry and their prospective colonels, and in the latter case money frequently changed hands. The colonel of *Piedmont,* for example, sold positions in his regiment "like meat in a butcher shop, lieutenants for a thousand *écus* and companies for two thousand. . . ." [10]

The functions of the colonel and captain were principally the direction and command of their units. The lieutenant colonel was second in command of the regiment, and often better versed in this matter than the colonel.[11] The major was the chief administrative officer and supervised the training of the troops.[12] The subaltern officers had no specialized functions, but were often detailed for recruiting purposes.[13]

Customarily the corps of officers is linked with the *noblesse d'épée,* and to a large degree the association is correct. The old nobility had been gradually replaced in public affairs and civil service by those of lesser birth, but it sought in the army its last refuge. "Here it defended its privileges with even more obstinacy, because it had the vague premonition that on this ground it was fighting its last battle." [14] The military profession was, after all, the one which had brought the old nobility into being, and the tradition was still strong in the eighteenth century. Indeed the feudal levy, the historic *arrière-ban,* was called for the last time in 1758 for coastal defense.[15]

The *noblesse de cour,* the great families who surrounded the monarch, were extremely successful in installing themselves in the upper echelons of the military hierarchy. Close to the fountain of preference, they let little escape them.

10. General Torcy to Belle-Isle, March 19, 1759, A¹ 3510–43.

11. In peacetime the colonel was required to spend only three months a year with his regiment, while the lieutenant colonel was always with the unit. Bacquet, *Infanterie,* pp. 14–15, 20.

12. On the major's functions, see Ray, *Réflexions,* p. 97; Mention, *Armée,* p. 102.

13. Bacquet, *Infanterie,* p. 27.

14. Mention, *Armée,* p. 1.

15. Louis Tuetey, *Les officiers sous l'ancien régime, nobles et roturiers* (Paris, 1908), p. 19.

The list of general and staff officers posted to duty in Germany in 1758 is almost a directory of the great noble families of France—the houses of Broglie, Noailles, Rohan, Ségur, Maupéou, etc. Among the 181 general officers there were 3 Princes of the Blood Royal, 5 other princes, 11 dukes, 44 counts, 38 marquis, 14 chevaliers, and 6 barons. Every name, without exception, bears the noble particle.[16]

In the cadres of *officiers particuliers* the young scions of the great families were in competition with the provincial nobility and the bourgeoisie. The provincial nobles had the advantage of their birth, but lacked wealth and powerful connections at court, and their advancement was painfully slow. One of the very few *hobereaux* who recorded his plight was Captain Jacques Mercoyrol de Beaulieu. His reminiscences betray what must have been a general bitterness and discouragement over the discrimination shown against the *noblesse de second rang*—many of whom, Mercoyrol tells us, were "worth more than some of our dukes." [17]

It is virtually impossible to establish with any accuracy the degree to which the bourgeoisie or *roturiers* succeeded in penetrating the corps of officers. In the eighteenth century it was very difficult to expose fraudulent nobility and today the task would be impossible. The fragmentary evidence seems to indicate a fairly high proportion of commoners, and modern estimates vary from one-third to one-half.[18] In spite of the prejudice against them, the *roturiers* could often bring into play an invaluable resource—money. The captain, for example, was often obliged to spend his own money for the upkeep of his company, and colonels were prone to forget their aristocratic scruples in favor of a prospective captain

16. "Etat de Mss. les Officiers Généraux, Brigadiers, officiers des Etats-Majors et autres employés à l'Armée du Bas Rhin pendant les six premier mois de 1758," Gayot MSS, 648–117.

17. *Campagnes,* p. 434. An excellent exposition of the state of the provincial nobility is found in Tuetey, *Officiers,* pp. 1–39.

18. Tuetey, *Officiers,* p. 99, n. 2; Henri Carré, *Louis XV* (Vol. VIII, Pt. 2 of *Histoire de France illustré depuis les origines jusqu'à la Révolution,* ed. Ernest Lavisse [Paris, 1911]), p. 228.

who could keep his company well.[19] Even if money were lacking the *roturier* could still hope for advancement, though the path was long and devious. From lieutenant one could move to the rank of major, which was equivalent to that of captain, but not costly. From here the aspiring officer could rise to lieutenant colonel, and finally brigadier, avoiding in the process the unattainable captaincy and colonelcy.[20] In the artillery and corps of engineers the chances for advancement were even better, since these services were those of "technicians" with special skills, and not so attractive to the nobility.[21]

A distinct class were the *officiers de fortune,* the rare individuals who had begun as common soldiers and risen through the ranks to obtain commissions. Their number was very limited, and once again they had a better chance in the artillery and engineers. They frequently made their goal a captaincy of grenadiers, for grenadiers were recruited without difficulty or great expense from the other companies in a regiment. The number of *officiers de fortune* was limited to six or seven in cavalry and infantry regiments, but in the artillery twenty-two were permitted per regiment.[22] Among the few *officiers de fortune* who rose to rank of general officer in the period was M. Guille, a brigadier in the corps of engineers.[23]

Only two officers of humble origins became really prominent and attained the rank of lieutenant general during the

19. Bacquet, *Infanterie,* p. 10. A widespread though rigorously condemned practice was that of the *concordat.* Wealthy officers contributed to a clandestine fund which became a "pension" for their superiors, actually a bribe to encourage their early retirement. "Lettre circulaire adressée à MMs. les colonels d'infanterie par le Maréchal de Belle-Isle," March, 1758, A¹ 3510–57. See also Audouin, *Administration,* III, 161.

20. Dussauge, *Etudes,* pp. 27–28.

21. Louis-Auguste le Pelletier, *Mémoires de Louis-Auguste le Pelletier, seigneur de Glatigny, lieutenant général dans les armées du roi, 1696–1769* (Paris, 1896), Introduction, p. xvi. Half of the artillery officers were commoners according to Albert Babeau, *La vie militaire sous l'ancien régime: Les officiers* (Paris, 1891), p. 77.

22. Tuetey, *Officiers,* p. 263.

23. Le Pelletier, *Mémoires,* Introduction, p. xvi.

period of the Seven Years' War, and in both cases the men were of extraordinary ability—Bourcet and Chevert. Bourcet was the author of a treatise on mountain warfare which much impressed Napoleon, and Chevert played a prominent role in the German campaigns of 1757–1762.[24]

If the bourgeoisie created for itself a place in the lower cadres, it did so in spite of official displeasure. It was felt in the ministry that a commission should not go to a commoner so long as there was a noble who desired it. Belle-Isle sent a circular letter to all infantry colonels urging them to give preference to the nobility, "that precious portion of the state, its strength and its support." [25] A short time later Belle-Isle made it known that "the King desires henceforth that the regiments which are most used in the war be commanded only by those of quality." In pursuance of this policy the *roturier* who was serving as lieutenant colonel in the *Volontaires de Flandre* was replaced by the Chevalier de Jaucourt, "of one of the first houses of Burgundy." [26]

There are no figures on the number of foreign officers in

24. Chevert was much revered in his time, and his epitaph, attributed to Diderot, is worthy of reproduction here:

Sans aieux, sans fortune, sans appui,
Orphelin dès l'enfance,
Il entra au service à l'age de onze ans;
Il s'éleva, malgre l'envie, à force de mérite
Et chaque grade fut le prix d'une action d'éclat.
Le titre seul de Maréchal de France
A manqué, non pas à sa gloire,
Mais à l'exemple de ceux qui le prendront pour modèle.

—*Biographie Universelle*, VIII, 113.

25. "Lettre circulaire adressée à Mms. les colonels d'infanterie par le maréchal de Belle-Isle," March, 1758, A¹ 3510–57.

26. Belle-Isle to the Marquis de Cadillac, March 18, 1759, A¹ 3542–115. The tendency to discriminate against commoners in the corps of officers was rather constant during the century, with one notable exception. The *ordonnance* of November 25, 1750, established a system by which nobility could be obtained through military service; but the conditions laid down were so complex that only some two hundred letters patent were issued from 1750 to 1789. The text of the *ordonnance* is reproduced in part in Tuetey, *Officiers*, pp. 263, 367–72. Only rarely were officers ennobled for distinguished service; such was the case of Jean-Baptiste Berthier, the father of Napoleon's chief of staff. Tuetey, pp. 400–401.

the French service, but they were undoubtedly very numerous. They filled the foreign regiments and even became general officers. Here we find such names at FitzJames, Milord Clare, and the Earl of Thomond—Irish or Jacobite in their extraction. The Swiss are represented by Courten and Planta; Bergh and d'Isselbach were among the frequent German names appearing on the rosters of general officers.[27] There is no evidence of jealousy or hostility toward these officers on the part of their French colleagues, but this is natural in a century during which the fires of xenophobia were banked.[28]

The mixture of various classes in the corps of officers was an obvious source of discord. Even the most reasonable of nobles held that "a commoner can serve the king in his army with as much honor as a gentleman of the highest antiquity, but he is not at all in his place." [29] Less charitable members of the *noblesse d'épée* went so far as to attribute the reverses of the war to the presence of the commoners.[30] Among the regimental officers, where the competition was most keen, the discord was also most severe. The regimental commanders fought bitterly against the introduction of *aides-major,* fearing that these posts would provide still more opportunities for *officiers de fortune.*[31] In 1760 a serious scandal was unearthed in the *Piedmont* regiment. One of the captains was the son of a wealthy ship chandler of Marseilles. His aristocratic colleagues borrowed heavily from him and refused to repay the loans. When the captain threatened to expose his debtors, he was found murdered in his tent.[32]

---

27. The more important officers of foreign origin are mentioned *passim* in Eugène Fieffé, *Histoire des troupes étrangères au service de France depuis leur origine jusqu'à nos jours et de tous les régiments levés dans les pays conquis sous la première république et l'empire* (Paris, 1854).

28. Captain Mercoyrol de Beaulieu provides the only exception; he attributed the thorny character of Saint Germain to his Spanish origin, an assertion utterly without foundation. Mercoyrol de Beaulieu, *Campagnes,* p. 280.

29. Anonymous memoir cited in Dussauge, *Etudes,* p. 225.

30. Tuetey, *Officiers,* p. 240.

31. Audouin, *Administration,* III, 198.

32. The incident is recounted in Westphalen, *Feldzüge,* IV, 167–68; and Mouffle d'Angerville, *Louis XV,* IV, 4–5.

The nobility spent fully as much time nursing animosities within its own ranks—animosities which were merely transferred from Versailles to the field. All too many of their personal letters reveal the bitter rivalries that divided them: "You cannot imagine," one of them confided, "what sort of fellow this little Caraman is; in truth it is shameful that he is placed in the rear on the communications, while the Turpins, the Melforts and a crowd of good-for-nothings and imbeciles are facing the enemy." [33] The fact that the corps of officers was not a homogenous mass, but broken into antagonistic classes and cliques, unquestionably had evil effects on the military establishment.[34]

The corps of officers were fully aware that they lived in an age of privilege; they bombarded the hard-pressed minister and commander with requests for special considerations and favors—requests that could not always be ignored, particularly if the petitioner were someone with influential connections. The multitude of officers who spent the exciting months of campaigning in the field had no desire to spend the inactive months in Germany, and as soon as the army entered winter quarters a mass exodus began. The ministry cut the winter duty list to the bone, but even this was insufficient.[35] Even before the Army of the Lower Rhine entered winter quarters in 1758, colonels and lieutenant colonels had begun to besiege their commander, who wrote to Versailles for instructions.[36] The minister replied that in principle these officers should remain at their posts, as was the custom when the army was on foreign soil, but that leaves could be given in special cases where it was "absolutely necessary." [37] Two

33. Baron de Besenval to Castries, July 18, 1759, A¹ 3519–24.
34. "Schliesslich aber ist nicht am wenigsten an dieser Stelle der Krankheitskeim zu suchen, der die Armee des Lilienbanners zersetzt hat." Delbrück, *Kriegskunst,* IV, 301.
35. In the Army of the Lower Rhine, only seven of the thirty-five lieutenant generals were retained in Germany during the winter of 1758–1759, and only fifteen of the fifty-seven *maréchaux-de-camp.* "Etat de Ms. les officiers généraux et des différents états-majors proposés pour être employés pendant l'hiver de 1758 à 1759" (no date), A¹ 3486–94.
36. Contades to Belle-Isle, Oct. 30, 1758, A¹ 3485–258.
37. Belle-Isle to Contades, Nov. 4, 1758, A¹ 3486–68.

weeks later the beleaguered minister sent new instructions
to give leaves to half of the colonels, adding that "there are
very few of them for whom the ladies of the court and Paris
have not made requests of me." [38] As a result the cadres were
insufficient for a winter campaign, always a possibility in this
period. In March, 1759, with the opening of the campaign
imminent, Broglie had only seven general officers to place in
the battle line, including himself. There was hardly a colonel
or a brigadier to be found in the army.[39] Needless to say, the
few who did remain were far from content with their lot.

The selection of officers for staff duty was also complicated
by personal considerations, and the number of personnel was
swollen far beyond rational limits. Although the abuse was
excessive, Louis' complacence led him to grant all the requests of his generals and post their protegés to staff duty.[40]
The court had its candidates too: "The Duchess of Orleans is
extremely eager that M. de Melfort enter the army staff." [41]
Similarly Paris Duverney desired a place in the cavalry staff
for his client, M. de Vieuville.[42]

The task of drawing up an order of battle could be successfully undertaken only if the commander kept in mind the
vagaries of his general officers; even then the success was
momentary, for with the arrival of new officers the whole task
had to be undertaken again. "The order of battle has appeared," wrote one officer, "but you will pardon me for not
giving the positions of the general officers. They will not be
there long." [43] One of Clermont's letters reveals graphically
the problems involved with the order of battle:

> M. de Randan wanted to return to the line. . . . M. d'Armen-
> tières found that it was disagreeable for him to be in the in-
> fantry *en second* under M. de Contades, and desired to be

38. Belle-Isle to Contades, Nov. 19, 1758, A¹ 3487–43.
39. Broglie to General d'Armentières, March 3, 1759, A¹ 3913–26.
40. Belle-Isle to Clermont, April 10, 1758, A¹ 3501–223.
41. Clermont to Belle-Isle, March 10, 1758, A¹ 3510–27.
42. Clermont to Belle-Isle, May 9, 1758, A² 37–108.
43. Castenau to Baron de Gaix, June 5, 1760, *Lettres*, p. 163.

moved to the cavalry. M. de Poyanne wanted to remain with the *Carabiniers,* that obliged me to move all the officers of the left and right wings and disrupted my plan to put the infantry officers with the infantry and the cavalry officers with the cavalry.[44]

Often the military chiefs went to unusual lengths to accommodate their officers. Perhaps only in the eighteenth century could a general have written to his foe such a letter as this:

I have a favor to ask of Your Highness. Would you have the goodness to return with a passport and on his parole the Marquis de Tasse, Cornet in the *Lameth* cavalry regiment, who was taken prisoner at Rosbach? This officer is a man of a very good family and will miss an important and advantageous marriage if his return to France is not facilitated, and you are too kind and too considerate not to procure this for him if it is possible for you to do so.[45]

The corps of officers made their influence felt most decisively in the matter of *grâces*—advancement, decorations, pensions, and all the other awards that a grateful monarch bestowed on his deserving servants.[46] After each engagement, victorious or otherwise, field commanders submitted long lists of officers who had been wounded or had especially distinguished themselves. More important, military chiefs both in Paris and in the field received a constant and heavy stream of petitions, pleas, demands, and outright threats from officers of all ranks whose appetite for preferment was seemingly insatiable: The Count of Saint Germain found it "insupportable" to be the seventh lieutenant general in a corps of sixteen battalions.[47] Monsieur de Montfort had to have a lieutenant

44. Clermont to Belle-Isle, June 15, 1758, A¹ 3503–141.
45. Clermont to Ferdinand, April 15, 1758, A¹ 3501–271. As might be expected, Ferdinand promised to do what he could. Ferdinand to Clermont, April 16, 1758, A¹ 3501–276.
46. The chief decoration was that of the Order of Saint Louis, which carried a modest pension. In addition the Order of Military Merit, reserved for Protestant officers, was created by the *ordonnance* of March 10, 1759.
47. Saint Germain to Paris Duverney, Aug. 16, 1757, *Correspondance Saint Germain–Paris Duverney,* I, 122.

colonelcy or he would retire at the end of the campaign.[48]
The pitiable Count of Champigneulles was sure that he had
more time in grade than any other general officer.[49] Monsieur
de Lanjamet required a promotion for himself and a colonelcy
and captaincy for his two sons; otherwise he would have
no recourse but to leave the service.[50] An obscure lieutenant colonel with more temerity than tact wrote directly to
the ministry:

> I hope you will not take it ill that I ask for the command of
> a brigade, but you will say, if you do me the honor of re-
> plying, that I should address myself to the general. I am not
> at all known to him, as I am only a lieutenant colonel.[51]

There was an unending search for a favorable endorsement
from a superior, or possibly a contact at the ministry itself.
Even a humble cornet like Castelnau wrote home suggesting
people whom his mother might work through to secure him
a lieutenancy from Madame de Pompadour.[52]

The ministry did its best to resist the flood of petitions and
the voluminous lists of *grâces* which followed every battle,
knowing full well that every officer who picked up "the
least scratch" got himself placed on the list.[53] In the promotions of general officers the ministry tried to take refuge in
the *ordre du tableau,* but with indifferent success. If the order
were observed with any rigor, it would have to be observed
in the question of command as well. In practice this was not
feasible; the able Broglie was given command while only
fifteenth on the list of lieutenant generals.[54] The influence of
certain officers transcended that of the minister himself. In
1759 the Saxon Count of Lusace, Louis' son-in-law, was
given command of a Saxon detachment and a lieutenant

48. General Cornillon to Belle-Isle, Aug. 6, 1758, A¹ 3480–73.
49. Champigneulles to Belle-Isle (no date), A¹ 3488–80.
50. Marquis de Saint Pern to Belle-Isle, March 3, 1759, A¹ 3513–17.
51. Petition of M. Dagière, June 27, 1758, A¹ 3477–194.
52. Castelnau to De Gaix, May 12, 1759, *Lettres,* p. 96.
53. Belle-Isle to Contades, Aug. 11, 1759, A¹ 3520–142.
54. Mercoyrol de Beaulieu, *Campagnes,* p. 252.

general's commission in accordance with an agreement signed with the Elector of Saxony. Immediately the two Princes of the Blood Royal, Condé and La Marche, raised such a clamor that they were also promoted to *maréchal-de-camp* in February, 1758, and lieutenant general six months later.[55]

Elsewhere the ministry also fought a losing battle. In March, 1758, some 129 brigadiers were issued letters of service for Clermont's army, which contained only about thirty brigades.[56] The ministry attempted to correct the error in May by issuing new letters of service, only thirty-three in number.[57] The reduction set off an explosion of wrath; the officers of the *Gendarmerie* sent the minister a memoir couched in the most indignant terms: "There is no one in the *Gendarmerie* to whom this disgrace is not personal, and who does not raise his voice to appeal to the justice and goodness of His Majesty." [58] By then the minister was in retreat; in July ten new brigadiers were named.[59] Another ministerial measure met a similar fate. A ruling of March, 1758, stated that no officer could aspire to the rank of colonel without seven years of previous service, five of them as captain.[60] Two months later the Count of Provence (the future Louis XVIII) became chief of the *Carabiniers* at the age of three.[61]

The ministry's efforts to slow down the rate of advancement was laudable, for the army already had far too many officers. In January, 1758, there were 16 marshals of France, 172 lieutenant generals, 176 *maréchaux-de-camp,* and 389 brigadiers.[62] Inexorably the number grew. One hundred and

55. See Belle-Isle's letter to Contades of Aug. 31, 1758, A^1 3481–237.

56. "Etat des brigadiers tant d'infanterie que de cavalerie et de dragons, dont Sa Majesté a resolu de se servir dans l'armée dont elle a donné le commandement à M. le Comte de Clermont, 11 mars 1758," A^1 3501–87.

57. *Etat* (no date), A^1 3505–129.

58. Memoir, Aug. 14, 1758, A^1 3505–96.

59. Belle-Isle to Contades, July 23, 1758, A^1 3479–182.

60. "Règlement que le Roy a juge à propos de faire sur l'ancienneté de service que doivent avoir les officiers qui seront proposés pour des regiments, mars 1758." A^1 3510–56.

61. Luçay, *Secrétaires d'état,* p. 316.

62. Dussauge, *Etudes,* p. 267.

twenty new lieutenant generals were created in the mass promotions of 1758, 1759, and 1762.[63] Colonels also proliferated, the majority of them having no regiments. By the end of Louis XV's reign there were nearly 900 colonels in an army which contained 163 regiments.[64] The number of captains increased also, but for a different reason. Since the cost of a company tended to increase, this unit became progressively smaller during the course of the century, and helped produce a larger proportion of officers to men. Already in 1740 the French Army was becoming marked in this respect, having one officer for every eleven soldiers, as against the Prussian ratio of one to twenty-nine.[65]

The hordes of general officers with the army were a source of continual embarrassment. A staff officer reported to the ministry that "what does the most harm is the quantity of useless and idle general officers; they set a bad example, voicing criticisms which their subalterns have adopted." [66] They swarmed about the headquarters in "tumultous assemblies," arguing, finding fault, and disrupting work.[67] When D'Estrées came from Paris to scold them for their disloyal attitude toward Contades, they ostentatiously absented themselves from a dinner given in D'Estrées's honor.[68]

The multitudes of general officers strained finances as well as discipline, for their salaries were princely even by eighteenth-century standards. The 182 general officers posted to Germany drew over half a million livres for six months of campaign duty—a sum that would have paid the wages of twenty thousand soldiers.[69] During the same six months they were entitled to draw over 900,000 forage rations and

63. Ray, *Réflexions*, p. 267.
64. Carré, *Louis XV*, p. 372.
65. Delbrück, *Kriegskunst*, IV, 268. See also Sautai and Desbrière, *Cavalerie*, pp. 2–3.
66. General Cornillon to Belle-Isle, Jan. 3, 1758, A¹ 3500–10.
67. Belle-Isle to Mortaigne, May 12, 1758, A¹ 3490–32.
68. Barbier, *Journal*, VII, 190.
69. Calculations based upon the *état* for 1758, A² 35–36.

1,170,000 rations of bread.[70] The luxury that surrounded general officers was a vice that plagued all armies,[71] but the French by their own admission were the worst in this respect;[72] a few comparative figures will bear this out. The British army, whose officers certainly lived well, allotted thirty men's rations to a lieutenant general, as against eighty for a French officer of the same rank.[73] In the field a Prussian *Generalmajor* could have no more than six guests at his table, nor serve more than six dishes. His French counterpart could entertain fourteen, and offer them as many as thirteen dishes in two courses.[74] Even this liberal allowance seemed "indecent" to many,[75] who spurned the ministerial injunction to follow "the example the King of Prussia gives us." [76] Servants abounded; the Duke of FitzJames, a lieutenant general, had twenty-eight.[77] Often there were as many as forty servants per regiment;[78] in the exclusive *Gendarmerie* there was a valet to serve every four soldiers.[79]

The historian Emile Léonard stresses the essentially non-professional nature of the corps of officers as one of its most important characteristics,[80] and this probably provides the chief reason for the widespread criticism concerning the

70. *Ibid.*
71. During the campaign of 1745 the Duke of Cumberland had one hundred and forty tons of personal baggage. Rex Whitworth, *Field Marshal Lord Ligonier: A Story of the British Army, 1702–1770* (Oxford, 1958), p. 96.
72. Richelieu to Paulmy, Dec. 23, 1757, A¹ 3446–30.
73. Whitworth, *Ligonier*, p. 95; *Etat*, A² 35–36.
74. Dussauge, *Etudes*, p. 281, n. 2; *Ordonnance du 2 juin 1758*. The same *ordonnance* prohibited silver services. In the spring of 1758 the Hanoverians seized some 600,000 livres worth of silverware in the baggage they captured. Westphalen to Haenichen, March 1, 1758, Westphalen, *Feldzüge*, II, 271.
75. Count de Guerchy to Belle-Isle, Aug. 5, 1758, A¹ 3480–75.
76. Belle-Isle to Mortaigne, March 3, 1758, A¹ 3490–10.
77. *Etat de la demande,* May, 1758, A¹ 3502–251 *bis.*
78. "Etat des cavaliers et soldats qui composent l'escorte des équipages aussi que les domestiques prenant pain et viande, des chevaux des officiers, et des equipages" (no date), A¹ 3506–87.
79. Ray, *Réflexions*, p. 196.
80. *Armée*, pp. 1–3.

officer's ignorance of his functions. What the average officer knew of his profession he had learned in the school of experience or by independent reading of books on the "military art." Though there had been sporadic attempts at establishing schools for prospective officers (and at peacetime maneuvers), the only officers formally trained there were artillerists and engineers. Paris Duverney was instrumental in founding the Ecole Militaire in 1751, but it came too late to have any salutary effect in this last major war of the old regime.

Broglie held that the chief fault of the military establishment was the "total ignorance, from the *sous-lieutenant* to the lieutenant general, of the duties of their post and all the details that concern it." [81] Two other eminent observers, Saint Germain and Guibert, echoed Broglie's complaints.[82] This situation was also encouraged by the evils of the system of advancement. The young Prince of Condé, whose meteoric rise to lieutenant general has already been noted, asked soon after his elevation for a mentor, for he desired to "learn the profession." [83] There were, indeed, officers who tried to supplement honor and bravery with knowledge; the hundreds of technical memoirs preserved in nearly all the archives of France attest to this. Most of them, however, were doomed to obscurity like M. Dom Germain, a man completely dedicated to his profession, but lacking the "resourcefulness to make himself noted, and therefore to advance." [84]

The government was very reluctant to remove bad officers, though it possessed the right to do so. The various *ordonnances* contained a rather complete system of military justice,

81. Broglie to the Abbé de Broglie, Aug., 1759, as cited in Broglie, *Secret,* I, 342.
82. See Guibert, *Tactique,* I, 231; and Saint Germain's "Mémoire sur les vices du militaire francais," in *Correspondance Saint Germain–Paris Duverney,* I, 197–212. Ligonier wrote disdainfully that "a man in the French Army is esteemed an officer so long as he dances, has a nice figure, and is a swordsman." Whitworth, *Ligonier,* p. 171.
83. Contades to Belle-Isle, Oct. 17, 1758, A¹ 3485–18. This was the same Prince of Condé who was to lead the army of *émigrés* some thirty years later.
84. Clermont to Belle-Isle, May 17, 1758, A¹ 3502–206.

but the application of the statutes was not uniform.[85] The ministry closed its eyes to much, but was occasionally jolted into action by some flagrant case of dereliction. When General Villemur displayed criminal negligence in allowing Ferdinand to cross the Rhine unopposed, his error could not pass unpunished. But since Villemur was a protegé of Paris Duverney, he was only recalled—"purely and simply to do nothing." [86] When the officers of the garrison at Minden signed a shameful capitulation which permitted them their liberty and made prisoners of their troops, they were all court-martialed and cashiered.[87] As a rule, the ministry seldom invoked the court-martial. It arrogated much disciplinary authority to the colonels, and some regiments had their own military police. The foreign regiments had their own system of justice with exclusive jurisdiction.[88]

The government made little headway in interfering with "questions of honor." The Court of the *Point d'Honneur,* a special tribunal composed of the Marshals of France, made some attempt to ajudicate these questions, but only the most sensational cases seem to have reached it.[89] Duels were still frequent. Two captains of the *Champagne* regiment, La Fenestre and D'Agay, had been mortal enemies for twenty-eight years, and had met seven times on the field of honor. La Fenestre had his head blown off by a cannon ball at Fillingshausen, but his partisans noted with a point of pride that a fragment of his skull put out D'Agay's right eye.[90]

85. The criminal regulations were not codified, but are found scattered through the *ordonnances,* many of which dated from the preceding century. A convenient digest of them is found *passim* in Nicolas d'Héricourt, *Elémens de l'art militaire* (Paris, 1756).

86. Belle-Isle to Clermont, June 6, 1758, A¹ 3477–2 *bis.*

87. Mouffle d'Angerville, *Louis XV,* III, 131.

88. Dussauge, *Etudes,* pp. 161, 172.

89. For a slap given without provocation the court inflicted a penalty of two years' confinement. If there was provocation the sentence was only one year in prison. Mention, *Armée,* p. 54. See further H. Pierquin, *La juridiction du point d'honneur et le tribunal des maréchaux sous l'ancien régime* (Paris, 1904).

90. Mercoyrol de Beaulieu, *Campagnes,* pp. 351–52.

In countless instances the corps of officers flouted regulations with impunity. In some cases necessity dictated their action; captains, for example, were so poorly paid that they could not maintain their companies without collecting the pay of non-existent soldiers, and a century of reiterated prohibitions never destroyed the practice.[91] Officers were required to wear the full breastplate or *cuirasse* in action, but it was a point of honor not to do so.[92] When the conservatism of the officers led them to nullify important efforts at reform, the result was much more serious; such was the case when many of them refused to adopt new drill methods based on the Prussian system.[93]

So far much has been said of the faults of the corps of officers, and little about their positive qualities. It must be said in their favor that in valor they were second to none. And when their efforts and sacrifices were largely in vain, they were not insensible to the fact that something was seriously wrong. But they never associated the problem with their own vices. If there was one basic fault with the cadres, it was the fact that their personal ambitions and desires were often incompatible with the general good, and the unreasoning insistence on the one was disastrous to the other. In their behalf it might be argued that in an age of privilege and preferment this incompatibility was difficult to see. In any event there were few who agreed with the obscure officer who wrote of his colleagues:

---

91. Bacquet, *Infanterie*, p. 7.
92. Belle-Isle's own son, the Count of Gisors, received a mortal wound leading a charge at Krefeldt; had he been wearing the *cuirasse,* it would probably have saved his life. Dussauge, *Etudes,* p. 245. The same distorted sense of honor could result in an almost criminal disregard for the lives of others. At Minden the Marquis de Saint Pern, commander of the *Grenadiers de France,* refused to let his men seek cover during a fierce bombardment, desiring to impress properly another detachment of grenadiers placed behind him. The *Grenadiers de France* needlessly lost two colonels and three hundred men. Alexandre-Marie-Léonor de Saint Mauris, prince de Montbarey, *Mémoires* (Paris, 1826–1827), I, 174.
93. Rousset, *Gisors,* p. 327.

The public good touches them only so far as their own good is completely included therein, and they count as nothing the harm they do to the affairs of our master, the loss of so many brave men and the ruin of an army, provided that they achieve their purposes.[94]

94. Castelnau to Baron de Massaguel, Aug. 13, 1759, *Lettres,* p. 114.

7

Personnel: The Soldiers

If the officers of the French army were essentially amateurs, the soldiers whom they led were not. The long period of training necessary, the large number of peacetime effectives, and the resultant policy of long-term enlistments tended to make the soldier of the old regime a professional. For most of the line regiments the recruiting regulations were uniform. They provided for voluntary enlistments for a period of six years; recruits were to be between the ages of sixteen and forty, at least five feet one inch in height, and of sufficient strength to support the rigors of the campaign.[1]

In wartime recruiting was usually done in the winter months, while the army was in quarters. Subaltern officers were detached for this duty and accordingly established themselves in what they hoped were fertile areas in idle manpower. In the village squares throughout France they could be found shaking their cash boxes and shouting the traditional cry "Who wants some?"[2] Some units engaged the services of professional recruiters, or *racoleurs,* who undertook to procure men at so much per head. Once the recruits had been enrolled, they were sent to border towns of eastern France, and periodically moved under escort to join the army and the regiments in which they had enlisted.[3]

1. *Ordonnance du 5 juillet 1760;* see also Comte R. de Sars, *Le recrutement de l'armée permanente sous l'ancien régime* (Paris, 1920), pp. 137–38. The system used for the militia, it should be noted, was based upon compulsory service. Since the militia's role in the field force was negligible, the institution will be referred to only incidentally. For further information concerning the militia, see Jacques Gebelin, *Histoire des milices provinciales (1688–1791). Le tirage au sort sous l'ancien régime* (Paris, 1882).

2. Sars, *Recrutement,* p. 126.

3. Customarily the contingents were dispatched to the army only when they had grown quite large. This simplified the problems of escort and

The recruiting system gave rise to many abuses, a situation that was applicable to Europe generally in that age. The professional recruiters who made their headquarters the Quai de la Feraille in Paris were the most serious offenders. Deception was widely practiced, and countless naïve souls signed the enlistment rolls in the belief that they were entering the service of some nobleman in the capacity of servant.[4] Although recruits were supposed to be examined by *commissaires des guerres* and other royal officials, there must have been considerable neglect in this regard. Late in 1757 it was discovered that a young girl had been enrolled in the *Enghien* regiment; the lady in question had served several months in the field before her sex was discovered.[5] The physician Colombier, who had served with the armies and knew whereof he spoke, found among recruits boys of thirteen and fourteen and the deaf, lame, and nearly blind.[6]

The system just outlined applied to most units, but by no means to all of them. It has already been noted that grenadier companies were recruited from the riflemen companies in the battalion itself, the grenadier captains paying twenty-five livres per head to the captains from whom the recruits were drawn.[7] The grenadier companies then supplied men for the *Grenadiers Royaux;* this latter unit was in turn the source of recruits for the *Grenadiers de France.*[8] In general the practice tended

---

transportation but often meant the new soldiers reached the army too late to be given much training before the campaign began. A detachment of eight thousand was sent to the Army of the Lower Rhine late in April, 1758, after the campaign had opened. Belle-Isle to Clermont, April 21, 1758, A¹ 3501–299.

4. For a description of various illicit practices in recruiting, see Capitaine Auguste-Philippe Herlaut, "Les abus de recrutement au XVIIIᵉ siècle," *Revue de XVIIIᵉ siècle*, I, No. 3 (juillet-septembre, 1913), 294–301.

5. Undated and unsigned memoir, A² 33–99.

6. Jean Colombier, *Code de médecine militaire pour le service de terre* (Paris, 1777), I, 153. Colombier devoted considerable space in his work to advice for recruiting officers; among other things he cautioned them against prospective recruits afflicted with bad breath, watery eyes, and baldness—this latter condition he considered a sign of incipient epilepsy (pp. 141–61).

7. D'Héricourt, *Elémens*, III, 245.

8. Gebelin, *Milices*, pp. 152–56.

to skim off the best men for service in the elite units, at the expense of uniform quality. The same practice existed to a lesser degree among the mounted units, where the *Carabiniers* were drawn from cavalry regiments.[9]

A special problem was posed by the numerous foreign regiments in French service; these comprised about a fifth of the regulars and were mainly infantry.[10] The Swiss regiments took care of their own recruiting, the practice being governed by long-standing capitulations between the units and the French government.[11] These Swiss regiments enjoyed the rare distinction of always having a full complement, or very near it.[12] It was impossible to keep the other foreign regiments at full strength by employing only the appropriate nationals in each case. Though the French government got permission from Vienna to recruit for its German regiments within the Empire, the practice was opposed by the local authorities, since it encouraged their own troops to desert to the French service.[13] Even Maria Theresa, normally eager to accommodate her chief ally, refused to permit the French to recruit in Hungary for the hussars.[14] As a result these normally Hungarian units came to contain many Frenchmen.[15] The

9. Sautai and Desbrière, *Cavalerie*, p. 14.

10. Comprising fourteen German regiments, thirteen Swiss, five Hungarian (hussars), five Irish, and one Scotch. See Fieffé, *Troupes étrangères*, pp. 268–78.

11. For further information regarding the status of the Swiss regiments, see the preface to Max Hoegger, "Die Briefe des Georg Leonhard Högger von St. Gallen, Hauptmann im Schweizerregiment Waldner im französichen Diensten an seinen Vetter Burgermeister Daniel Högger in St. Gallen," *Neujahrsblatt der Feuerwerken Gesellschaft (Artillerie-Kollegium) in Zurich*, CXXXXVII (1956); and Hubert Elie, "Le marquis de Courteille, ambassadeur de Louis XV en Suisse, et le recrutement des troupes suisses au service de la France," *Revue historique de l'armée*, X, No. 4 (1956), 5–22.

12. "Ils ont toujours été les plus forts." Belle-Isle to Contades, May 7, 1759, A^1 3515–64.

13. "Mémoire remise par M. le Vice-Chancellier à son Excellence M. le Cte. de Choiseul, Ambassadeur de France" (no date), A^1 3518–67.

14. Dussauge, *Etudes*, p. 173.

15. This admixture does not seem to have lessened the foreign flavor of the hussars. French recruits soon acquired the habit of swearing in Magyar. Fieffé, *Troupes étrangères*, p. 279.

German regiments recruited heavily from the provinces of Alsace and Lorraine, and the Irish units customarily filled their ranks from the inhabitants of the region around Saint Omer.[16]

Which classes in French society supplied the soldiers of the old regime? Contemporaries held that the army was composed of the scum of the nation.[17] Some modern authorities are inclined to describe those who succumbed to the recruiting officer's entreaties in similarly unflattering terms: idlers, beggars, vagabonds, dispossessed peasants, jailbirds, etc.[18] Other military historians have attempted to challenge the traditional view.[19] In truth, neither argument has been supported by any systematic research. Fortunately the question can now be answered, thanks to Professor Corvisier's recent study of the soldier of the old regime, a definitive work in the tradition of French scholarship.[20]

Corvisier finds that every class in the nation was represented in the ranks. The number drawn from the nobility was admittedly small; the *classes populaires*—ranging from butchers to day laborers—was about 84 per cent. Misery alone did not drive men into the army. The more destitute portions of France did not consistently supply more recruits than the prosperous regions. The urban element in the ranks was about a third, considerably greater than its proportion of the general population. Professor Corvisier has been able to substantiate statistically the traditional view that a heavy proportion of the troops came from the frontier provinces of the north and east. On the other hand he has demolished the contention that hordes of ex-valets and other *domestiques*

16. Dussauge, *Etudes,* p. 200; Mention, *Saint Germain,* p. 136.
17. Comte de Saint Germain, *Mémoires* (Amsterdam, 1779), p. 183; Guibert, *Tactique,* I, 14.
18. Mention, *Armée,* p. 11.
19. See, for example, Hennet, *Regards,* pp. 8–9.
20. André Corvisier, *L'Armée française de la fin du XVII° siècle au ministère de Choiseul: Le soldat* (Paris, 1964). This work may be consulted with profit on virtually every aspect of the soldier's life.

brought their libertine ways to the army; they figure for less than 1 per cent.[21] Certainly one can no longer equate the common soldier with the eighteenth-century proletariat without considerable qualification.

The armies of the old regime, like all armies, knew the dangers of employing green troops without battle-hardened veterans to leaven the mass. Though the process of training was a rather informal affair left largely to regimental officers or even non-commissioned officers, it was nonetheless a matter of vital importance. In the eighteenth century the evolutions were intricate and took much practice. The manual of arms was also complicated—muskets were charged in twelve cadenced steps.[22] Saint Germain estimated that it took six years to form a soldier completely, and that a battalion should have no more than a third of its men green, otherwise it would not be "solid." [23] This is the reason behind the strenuous efforts which the government made to lure deserters back to the ranks, and to secure prompt release of those taken prisoner. After much effort an agreement was reached with Ferdinand for the prompt exchange of prisoners, and the French willingly paid a "ransom" of eleven livres per head for any excess of French soldiers.[24] Belle-Isle estimated that the returned prisoners would be worth twice their number in recruits.[25]

Although the eighteenth century was a stranger to the modern concept of *guerre à l'outrance,* the military establishment had a heavy consumption of manpower. It was estimated that an army on war footing would lose about one-fifth of its strength from non-combat causes (desertion, illness, etc.) each year, and with a peak force of 330,000 men

21. *Ibid.,* pp. 473–510 *passim.*
22. Mention, *Saint Germain,* p. 199. For a highly critical description of training methods, see Guibert, *Tactique,* I, 155.
23. "Mémoire sur les vices du militaire français," *Correspondance Saint Germain–Paris Duverney,* I, 204.
24. "Traité et convention pour les malades, blessés, et prisonniers de guerre," October 19, 1757, Westphalen, *Feldzüge,* III, 60–65.
25. Belle-Isle to Contades, Sept. 25, 1758, A¹ 3483–171.

this would mean nearly 50,000 replacements per year exclusive of battle casualties.[26]

The forces fielded by France in the years 1757–1762 were actually rather modest, considering the population of the realm. At maximum strength there were slightly under 330,000 men in line units, and approximately 80,000 in the militia—a total force of about 400,000 men. This figure does not compare favorably with the maximum armed strength of 450,000 men in the reign of Louis XIV when the population was perceptibly smaller.[27] These figures are certainly open to challenge and are probably excessive; statistics on the actual number of men under arms were very often deliberately falsified. But there is further indication of a relative decline in military manpower and in the ability to obtain it. The figures for the numbers of men which the government thought it could raise and called for are highly instructive. During the thirteen years of the War of the Spanish Succession the government sought 655,000 regular troops, both French and foreign, the annual average being about 50,000. In the War of the Austrian Succession the call was for 345,000, or about 49,000 annually. For the Seven Years' War the government sought 270,000, about 38,000 annually.[28] In each case the figures represent replacement or increase to the standing army at the commencement of hostilities, but comparison is still suggestive, particularly when viewed against the background of an increasing population.

The French utilization of manpower also shows up very poorly when compared to the effort made by other belligerents. England, with a population of perhaps eight million and a large naval establishment, fielded 140,000 men (army and marines).[29] In France the military took approximately every

26. Sars, *Recrutement*, p. 134.

27. Albert Babeau, *La vie militaire sous l'ancien régime: Les soldats* (Paris, 1891), pp. 13–14.

28. The figures are those given in Corvisier, *Soldat*, pp. 157–58.

29. Whitworth, *Ligonier*, p. 246. The figure does not include subsidized German troops.

eleventh man between the ages of nineteen and forty-five. In Hanover, Hesse, Brunswick, and the Prussian domains, every fourth or fifth man in the same age group was called to the colors.[30]

The French policy might have found justification if the authorities had committed themselves to Marshal Saxe's dictum that battles were won by small armies but good ones. This was not the case, however.[31] The war machine was, in fact, straining under its maximum effort. As early as 1758 there developed a manpower crisis, and the minister declared "our realm is becoming exhausted in men";[32] a disturbingly large proportion of recruits were being rejected as unfit for duty.[33] In 1760 the recruits arrived late, and in insufficient quantities. Most of them were deserters who immediately decamped again, often taking horses with them.[34] The hard-pressed government turned to the dangerous practice of using militiamen to fill the depleted ranks of the line regiments, and nearly thirteen thousand were used for this purpose.[35] In some companies as many as a third of the soldiers were from the militia, and the proportion of green troops reached 50 per cent.[36]

The French were much impressed by the ruthless manner with which Frederick forced subject populations into the ranks of his armies, and orders were issued in 1759 to utilize the militia of Hanau, a Prussian dependency then in French hands. The local authorities were dragooned into proclaiming the levy, but on the appointed day not a single militiaman appeared; they had all gone into hiding or passed into enemy lines.[37] Attempts to enroll twelve hundred volunteers in Hanau met with the same failure, though the authorities were in-

30. Westphalen, *Feldzüge*, I, 88–89; Delbrück, *Kriegskunst*, IV, 304.
31. Saint Germain maintained to the contrary: "On a cru pouvoir réparer par la quantité le défaut de la qualité, et l'on s'est trompé." "Vices du militaire français," *Correspondance Saint Germain–Paris Duverney*, I, 208.
32. Belle-Isle to Contades, Nov. 19, 1758, A¹ 3487–108.
33. Crémilles to Clermont, May 6, 1758, A² 37–108.
34. Broglie to Belle-Isle, May 29, 1760, A¹ 3554–295.
35. Gebelin, *Milices*, p. 204.
36. Mercoyrol de Beaulieu, *Campagnes*, pp. 175–76.
37. Broglie to Belle-Isle, May 3, 1759, A¹ 3515–22.

structed to proceed with "all of the Prussian vigor."[38] Such methods made no headway against the "invincible repugnance" of the German populations.[39] The French regiments were given special permission to incorporate as many as five enemy deserters into each company, in the fond hope that these could be attracted to the French service.[40] Late in 1758 agents were sent into enemy territory to distribute handbills which offered Hanoverian soldiers a cash bonus and their old rank if they would "pass into the service of a foreign power" which would receive them "with open arms." The handbills painted the French service in the most glowing terms: "You will have to fear neither whippings nor Prussian rigor, nor want, nor unnecessary exertions, nor any diminution or deduction in your pay."[41] Despite the elaborate promises the deserters never came.[42]

There were several reasons why the army was hard-pressed for men while the country abounded in them. The system of voluntary enlistment was a handicap, and the government had sufficient regard for public opinion to prevent wholesale abuses.[43] There was little incentive to join the ranks, and certainly no great wave of patriotic fervor. The war was

38. Belle-Isle to Contades, May 7, 1759, A[1] 3515–64.
39. Paulmy to Clermont, Feb. 24, 1758, A[2] 35–90.
40. "Agenda pour S.A.S." (no date), A[2] 35–1.
41. The handbill further promised that deserters could pass into the French lines with absolute safety if they wore white cockades in their hats. "Avis à tous les officiers et soldats de l'armée hanovrienne" (no date) A[1] 3511–12 *bis.*
42. "Il n'arrive toujours aucuns déserteurs des enemis avec des cocardes blanches. Il vient quelques Hanovriens à Dusseldorff sans cocardes blanches, qui sont en mauvais état pour leur habillement." Contades to Belle-Isle, Jan. 15, 1759, A[1] 3511–109. Most of the French agents seem to have been intercepted before they could complete their mission. See Westphalen to Haenichen, Jan. 26, 1759, *Feldzüge,* III, 139.
43. There are numerous instances of individuals pressured into enlistment, and subsequently released by ministerial intervention. See Herlaut, "Les abus de recrutement." An anonymous memoir on recruiting opposed impressment with Machiavellian logic: "Il faut toujours conserver un esprit de liberté chimérique dans la nation, lequel esprit engendre les sentiments d'honneur; mais si la liberté avait quelque chose de réel, elle menerait à la révolte." "Projet à exécuter des à present mais encore avec plus d'aisance si l'on venait à faire la paix" (no date), A[1] 3548–90.

manifestly unpopular with many of the intelligentsia, who admired Frederick and called themselves "Prussians." It would be exceedingly difficult to prove that this attitude percolated down into the masses, for they were largely inarticulate; nevertheless this possibility cannot be ignored. Certainly this war was less personal to the average Frenchman than to his opponents across the channel or across the Rhine. For England the dark days of 1756 and 1757 and the dynamic leadership of Pitt could serve as catalysts in galvanizing the nation to action. The Hanoverian or Hessian had the conviction that in repelling the traditional invader he was defending his own hearth and home. The "Prussian fanaticism" of the German populations that so puzzled the French was more likely the first stirrings of a nascent German nationalism.

There are other more concrete reasons for the French manpower difficulties. At first the regular army had to compete with the large militia—some one hundred thousand men were raised in the levies of 1756, 1757, and 1758. In an attempt to ease the competition the ministry made no militia levies after 1758.[44] The system by which the regiments sought their own recruits worked fairly well in peacetime but failed as the war continued. The needed replacements were greater and the few officers detached for the service failed to fill up the ranks. In the spring of 1760 the ministry collected a motley crew of "vagabonds" which it offered to hard-pressed recruiters.[45] Later the same year the regiments were temporarily relieved of recruiting, and the task was assigned to the provincial intendants.[46] At the end of the war the new policy was retained.[47]

Another problem was that of money, or rather the lack of it. The government had great difficulty in providing the 125

44. Gebelin, *Milices,* p. 110.
45. Bourcet, *Mémoires,* I, 270–71.
46. *Ordonnance du 5 juillet 1760; Ordonnance du 25 novembre 1760.* See also Bacquet, *Infanterie,* p. 46; and Sars, *Recrutement,* p. 136.
47. *Ordonnance du 10 décembre 1762; Ordonnance du 21 décembre 1762.* See also Sars, *Recrutement,* p. 147.

livres allotted to infantry captains to cover the costs of enrolling a recruit, an allotment which was manifestly insufficient.[48] Regulations provided for an enlistment bounty of
thirty livres. The sum was too low to attract many recruits,
the actual "going price" being two or three times this amount.[49]
The regimental authorities themselves had to make up the
difference, a practice which often obliged them to go into
debt.[50] Another evil consequence of this state of affairs was
that it always kept the army at less than full strength. In order
to make both ends meet the captains had no choice but to
keep their companies under-strength, concealing the *non-
complet* by carrying non-existent soldiers on the rolls, and
"borrowing" soldiers to deceive inspectors when their companies were reviewed.[51] The official figures of effective
strength were therefore notoriously inaccurate, and the field
commander was reduced to guessing the size of his own
army.[52]

The soldier's profession was not an attractive one. French
society was, after all, far from being militaristic. It was a
serious breach of court etiquette to appear at Versailles in
uniform.[53] Among the population generally the soldier was
classed among the "vilest and most miserable citizens"; [54] on

48. Bacquet, *Infanterie,* p. 5.
49. Sars, *Recrutement,* pp. 137–39.
50. Castelnau's brother, De Gaix, purchased a company in 1760 for 7,000
livres; after two winters and three campaigns, he was in debt for over 5,000
livres. Castelnau, *Lettres,* p. 20. In 1759 the cavalry regiments of the Army
of the Lower Rhine were in debt 700,000 livres, and asking the ministry to
come to their rescue; otherwise they felt it would be impossible to restore
their depleted ranks. Comte de Fumel to Belle-Isle, Aug. 13, 1759, A¹ 3520–
207.
51. This practice was also known in the British army, but there it had
characteristically become a hallowed tradition. Each regiment of foot was
permitted to carry on its rolls six fictitious "warrant men"; their wages were
used to defray regimental expenses for recruiting, purchases of clothing, etc.
Edward E. Curtis, *The Organization of the British Army in the American
Revolution* (New Haven, 1926), p. 12.
52. This was the subject of much acrimonious correspondence with
Versailles. See for example Belle-Isle to Broglie, March 26, 1759, A¹ 3513–
196.
53. Léonard, *Armée,* p. 2.
54. Guibert, *Tactique,* I, 164.

the eve of the Revolution the public gardens of Paris still displayed signs prohibiting "dogs, street-walkers, lackeys, and soldiers." [55] Professor Corvisier has been able to show in his study that men from "respectable" families undoubtedly regarded the soldier's profession as an honorable one. He also claims to detect a less hostile attitude to the profession during the latter half of the century, and finds evidence of sympathy and even admiration for the soldier in the literature of the period.[56] Yet in the works of the major literary figures of the age—Voltaire's *Candide* and in England Smollett's *Roderick Random,* to cite but two—the picture of military life is anything but flattering. It is doubtful if the French soldier found an apologist of the first rank in literature before the publication of Alfred de Vigny's *Servitude et grandeur militaires* in 1835.

None but the most destitute could have been attracted to the ranks by the pay, though it was on a par with that of most other armies.[57] The common soldier's daily wage on campaign was five sous, eight deniers, being somewhat higher than garrison or winter quarter pay.[58] But part of the pay was withheld for the bread supplied by the *munitionnaire;* there were deductions for clothing and necessary expenses for tobacco, polish, hair powder, etc. The average soldier was left about two sous which he could call his own. If this were scrupulously saved for a year it would come to thirty livres—the price of a good suit of clothes.[59]

The common soldier's few rights were constantly abridged in spite of the stipulations of the *ordonnances* and the enlistment contract. Although his enlistment was for six years, there was no guarantee that he would be released at the expiration of that time. Regulations stated that only the two

55. Mention, *Armée,* p. 37.
56. *Soldat,* pp. 82–88.
57. The English army was probably the best paid in Europe. See Whitworth, *Ligonier,* p. 246.
58. In the then current monetary system the livre was composed of twenty sous, and the sou of twelve deniers. Regarding pay scales, see Babeau, *Soldats,* pp. 116–17; Corvisier, *Soldat,* pp. 826–27.
59. Based on the figures given in Babeau, *Soldats,* pp. 103, 107.

oldest soldiers per company could be released each year.[60] There were cases in which soldiers enrolled in 1758 were not released until 1766.[61] The *ordonnances* provided that a small number of soldiers could be given winter leave, but this was seldom granted since the captains gave leaves to fictitious soldiers to help conceal their deficiencies in men.[62]

It would be wrong to assume, however, that the soldier was prey to all the whims of his officers. The soldier was valuable property, difficult and expensive to replace, and it was to the company commander's own interest to preserve his "people." [63] This relationship was a positive advantage for both parties when the soldier ran afoul of military law. The *ordonnances* provided the death penalty for numerous offenses, from deserting to "marauding," and cruel or maiming punishments for many others.[64] If the transgressor were unlucky enough to be seized by the army's *prévôté* or military police, and thus brought to the attention of the commander, the penalty was apt to be severe. When four cavalrymen were apprehended outside the picket lines, they were automatically assumed to be up to no good, and Contades had them draw lots to see which one would be hanged.[65] If, however, the crime were punished by the unit commander the penalty was apt to be much less severe, though painful and humiliating. The culprit was often condemned to sit on a saw-horse for several hours with cannon balls tied to each leg, or to run the gauntlet of his fellows, who whipped him

60. Bacquet, *Infanterie,* p. 45.

61. Gebelin, *Milices,* p. 205, n. 2.

62. Mention, *Saint Germain,* p. 103, n. 1.

63. Mercoyrol de Beaulieu, *Campagnes,* p. 252.

64. In this supposedly enlightened age the old custom of piercing the tongue with a red-hot iron was still prescribed for blasphemy. *Ordonnance du 25 juin 1759.* See further D'Héricourt, *Elémens,* III, 68–109. Soldiers in other armies were no better off. The Prussian service was noted for the savagery of its discipline; Curtis cites cases of British soldiers condemned to 800 and 1,000 lashes. *British Army,* p. 28.

65. Contades to Belle-Isle, Aug. 1, 1758, A¹ 3480–18. Belle-Isle thought the judgment too liberal, and suggested that all four should have been strung up. Belle-Isle to Contades, Aug. 4, 1758, A¹ 3480–45.

with iron ramrods or shoulder straps from their muskets.[66] The prevailing attitude that the soldier "belonged" to his captain rebounded to his advantage in another way. An officer of another unit seldom dared reprimand him, whatever the gravity of his offense.[67]

The offense most often mentioned in the official correspondence was *la maraude*—theft and plundering from the local population for the purpose of obtaining what have been euphemistically called "supplementary field rations." When the supply system failed, as it did on occasion, the army's leaders took a realistic view and turned a blind eye to the depredation of troops driven by sheer necessity. This was the case in the final months of 1757, when the Army of the Lower Rhine was nearly destitute. Richelieu, who commanded on that occasion, was given the nickname of *Père la maraude* because of his complacence in this regard.[68]

In the eighteenth century desertion was endemic in all armies, and reached appalling proportions in wartime. Unfortunately exact figures are not available for the French armies. The *états* of army strength were deliberately falsified, as noted previously, and the number of deserters was probably much greater than that reported.[69] Ferdinand's secretary, usually well informed, estimated that the French had more

66. Running the gauntlet was also the penalty used for camp followers and was considered a dishonor; hence a curious custom arose: a soldier who had run the gauntlet had the regiment's flag passed over him to "purify" him. Mention, *Armée*, p. 65.

67. "Aucun officier n'oserait dire un mot aux soldats d'une autre troupe." "Mémoire sur les vices du militaire français," *Correspondance Saint Germain–Paris Duverney*, I, 174.

68. Duclos, *Mémoires*, II, 287. Even when the official attitude was less favorable the troops knew when to take advantage of opportunities. Just before Minden was abandoned in 1758 the garrison broke into the storage depot and stole "shoes, tents, arms, indeed everything in the magazine, even down to the planks which fenced it off." The *commissaire des guerres* who was trying to evacuate these supplies was forced to flee for his life. M. d'Erville to Gayot, July 8, 1758, Gayot MSS, 646–186.

69. In February, 1758, when Clermont was insisting that he had no more than 30,000 foot soldiers, the *état* showed 50,279 infantrymen present and in condition to bear arms, 1,571 on leave, 14,000 in the hospitals, and 3,051 deserters. "Etat de la composition des régiments d'infanterie de l'Armée du Bas Rhin commandée par M. le Cte. de Clermont au premier février 1758," A² 35–63.

than two thousand deserters in the first month of the campaign of 1759.[70] Great numbers sought refuge in the neutral Netherlands, where an observer estimated in 1760 that there were twelve thousand.[71] Many deserted one regiment for another, collecting an enlistment bonus in the process. Some thirty-four were discovered in one battalion of *Royal Deux Ponts*.[72] Both Frederick and Maria Theresa offered a bonus to deserters with no questions asked.[73] As a result many enterprising soldiers went back and forth from one service to another.[74]

The desperate ministry threatened deserters with summary execution, and then nullified this measure by granting amnesties in hopes of luring them back.[75] Great care was taken to reduce the opportunities to desert. When the army marched, it was followed by a detachment of the *prévôté,* which gathered up stragglers. In 1760 the *prévôté* was ordered to escort all troops moving within the realm as well.[76] When the army was encamped the area was cordoned off and continually patrolled.[77] The camp was never placed near a wooded area for the same reason.[78] Whenever the army moved, in France or in Germany, the civilian population was

70. Westphalen to Haenichen, May 7, 1759, *Feldzüge,* III, 256.

71. Memoir of Comte d'Onoy, accompanying Broglie's letter to Belle-Isle, May 2, 1760, A¹ 3554–23. Ferdinand advertised for these deserters in Dutch newspapers. Westphalen to Haenichen, Jan. 20, 1759, *Feldzüge,* III, 124.

72. "Liste des déserteurs français qui se trouvent engagés pour le 4ᵉ bataillon de Rᵃˡ Deux Ponts" (no date), A¹ 3502–133.

73. The ministry learned in 1759 that Austrian regiments were enrolling French deserters who arrived still wearing their uniforms; a stiff protest was sent to Vienna. Belle-Isle to Choiseul, July 16, 1759, A¹ 3519–1.

74. After much negotiation with the Russians, the government gathered up a large quantity of French deserters in Poland, only to discover that most of them could not be brought back. They could not pass through the Empire because they had also deserted from the Austrian service. M. de Mesnages to Belle-Isle, Feb. 6, 1759, A¹ 3912–29.

75. *Ordonnance du 10 juillet 1758,* "pour permettre aux soldats, cavaliers et dragons qui ont déserté avant le 1 février 1757 de s'engager indistinctement dans toutes les troupes de Sa Majesté, pour jouir de l'amnistie."

76. Audouin, *Administration,* III, 218–19.

77. See, for example, the elaborate measures taken by the Duc de Brissac, described in his letter to Belle-Isle of May 19, 1759, A¹ 3516–58.

78. Mention, *Armée,* p. 56.

warned of severe penalties for harboring deserters, and encouraged to turn them in by the promise of a reward.[79] Despite these elaborate measures desertion continued apace.

Several historians have attempted to penetrate the personality of the soldier of the old regime, but in this respect he will probably always remain faceless. During the course of months of bibliographical work and a year of archival research for the present study, not one letter written by a common soldier was found. What is known about him is largely what was said about him by his officers, and the image they projected was often distorted. The testimony is often contradictory. The Count of Saint Germain wrote:

> I lead a band of thieves, assassins fit for the rack who will turn tail at the first musket shot, and who are always ready to revolt. There has never been anything to equal it. The King has the worst infantry under the sun, and the most undisciplined. It is impossible to serve with such troops.[80]

Unquestionably Saint Germain painted too dark a picture; but then he was still smarting from the humiliating defeat at Rosbach, where everyone was seized with panic, from the commander on down. Most other officers were ready to concede that the French soldier was prone to indiscipline and *la maraude,* but Saint Germain's charge of cowardice finds practically no echo. In fact there is only one instance in which French troops displayed a singular lack of bravery— when a detachment under Chevert failed to seize a bridgehead in 1758. Even here the probable cause was the heavy number of green militiamen being employed.[81]

79. In Germany a very substantial reward of fifty livres was offered. Brissac to Clermont, April 12, 1758, A² 40–178.

80. Saint Germain to Paris Duverney, Nov. 11, 1757, *Correspondance Saint Germain–Paris Duverney,* I, 158.

81. "Pour mon malheur j'avais à commander des troupes dont il ne m'est guère possible de vous dire du bien, et pour comble d'infortune j'avais avec moi, et j'avais pris à Wesel plus de trois mil hommes de milices ou de nouvelles levées." Chevert to Belle-Isle, Aug. 5, 1758, A¹ 3480–66. The minister agreed that Chevert's force was "un ramassis peu propre à donner un coup de collier." Belle-Isle to Contades, Aug. 12, 1758, A¹ 3480–181.

By contrast there were countless instances in which the soldier could be seen at his best. When Hirschfeld was under siege in 1762 the sick and wounded of the garrison clamored for permission to leave their beds and join their comrades on the ramparts.[82] When the officers of the Minden garrison signed the shameful capitulation previously referred to, an unknown sergeant refused to be party to the agreement, and led over two hundred men back to the French lines.[83] All too rarely does the historian catch a glimpse of the common soldiers, serving with constancy in the most cruel conditions: wading for miles in knee-deep water, following the track which the artillery caissons broke in the ice, or hacking at the frozen earth with hatchets in order to drive their tent pegs.[84] The Chevalier de Ray, looking back on several decades of military service, concluded: "I rejoice in my fate, which destined me to command such men." [85]

82. Mercoyrol de Beaulieu, *Campagnes,* p. 406.
83. This incident is recounted in Belle-Isle's letter to Clermont of March 29, 1758, A¹ 3473–220. Louis himself ordered a diligent search for the heroic sergeant, but his identity was never discovered.
84. Mercoyrol de Beaulieu, *Campagnes,* pp. 161, 166.
85. *Réflexions,* p. 11.

8

Finances

Nowhere does the student of the old regime move with greater trepidation than through the murky waters of public finance. Much documentary material was destroyed in the upheavals of 1791 and 1871, and the loss is irreparable. Added to this are the almost insurmountable difficulties presented by the complicated and inaccurate accounting practices then current. The system was equally difficult for the minister of Louis XV, though this is a meager consolation for the modern researcher.[1]

The old regime did not operate on a budget as that term is understood today. The government could only estimate in the vaguest way its revenues or expenditures, and the errors were sometimes very great. The anticipated deficit for 1758 was 133,000,000 livres, but this proved 84,000,000 livres too low.[2] What the government lacked was an *état au vrai,* or real statement of expenses and revenues. This was not available, except long after the fiscal year had ended. The various disbursing officers were given two years to submit their accounts, and the period was extended to three years in wartime. In many cases this deadline was not met. The accounts of the *extraordinaire des guerres* for 1758 were not closed until 1766; those of the artillery for 1758 were not submitted to the auditing body, the Chambre des Comptes, until 1770.[3]

1. An excellent introduction to this subject is found in the opening chapters of the first volume of Marcel Marion's *Histoire financière de la France depuis 1715* (Paris, 1914).

2. Henri Martin, *Histoire de France* (4th ed., Paris, 1860), XV, 558.

3. Mention, *Armée,* p. 247.

The origin of the various revenues, if not their amounts, could generally be established. In the case of expenditures, however, the destination or governmental department to which they should be attributed was frequently not known. This situation arose from the widespread use of the *ordonnancement au comptant*. This pay order was originally used by the monarch for "secret" expenses whose nature could not be revealed for reasons of state. The *ordonnancement* therefore indicated neither the destination nor the recipient, but bore simply the royal notation "I know the purpose of this expenditure." Under Louis XV it became one of the chief methods of disbursement, with the sums outstanding reaching over 100,000,000 livres.[4]

Lacking any accurate knowledge of their financial state, the ministers of the old regime relied upon a theoretical or "model" budget, representing approximately the ordinary or peacetime income and expenditure. Added to this questionable set of figures was the "extraordinary" budget, incidental to the war. One such model budget places the normal revenues from all sources at 265,600,000 livres and total expenditures at 237,060,000 livres, leaving a sizable but fictitious surplus. The appropriation of the army was 84,000,000 livres; the navy received 25,000,000 livres; and 45,000,000 livres were allotted for debt service.[5]

This dubious set of statistics served as the foundation to which were added the *affaires extraordinaires,* the special finance operations resulting from the war. A statement of extraordinary expenditures is unfortunately lacking, but a tabulation of the extraordinary revenues exists in the form of an anonymous memoir. This compilation shows that during the seven years from 1756 through 1762 the government raised by various expedients 1,105,616,261 livres. The largest sum was raised in 1760—212,623,900 livres. Thereafter the extraordinary revenue fell to 183,870,787 livres in 1761 and 158,030,787 livres in 1762.[6]

The same obscurity which shrouds the fiscal transactions of the government generally also makes it difficult to penetrate the financial aspects of military administration. As might be expected, there are no authoritative figures of the budget for the ministry during the war. The budget for 1758 has been placed variously at 160,000,000 and 168,000,000 livres.[7] Choiseul states that the proposed military expenditures for 1761 were 180,000,000 livres.[8] Unsatisfactory as these figures are, they do permit the conclusion that the annual expenditures probably ranged between 150,000,000 and 200,000,000 livres.

The fiscal organization of the ministry of war was exceedingly complicated. Originally the normal military budget was small and regular, a result of the modest standing armies maintained in earlier centuries. This budget was called the *ordinaire des guerres,* and in time of war a second fiscal authority was established to cover the expenses of additional troops—the *extraordinaire des guerres.* During the seventeenth and eighteenth centuries the military expenditures increased rapidly, but the old system of dual accounting persisted. Since the *ordinaire* was a stable revenue of about 10,000,000 livres, it gradually became a small fraction of the military expenditures applied to the maintenance of the *maison du roi* or household troops. The vast bulk of the ministry's appropriation, both in peace and in war, still went

6. "Etat actual des affaires générales concernant les finances du Royaume de France qui constate, 1° les revenues et dépenses du Roy, 2° les affaires extraordinaires faittes en France depuis et compris l'année 1756 jusqu'en 1763, 3° les affaires particulières qui se font annuellement dans le royaume en faveur de la Cour de Rome, des évêques, des ducs, comtes et pairs," Bibliothèque de l'Arsenal, MS 4066A.

7. Audouin, *Administration,* III, 159; Silhouette's memoir in Charles-Joseph Mathon de la Cour, *Collection des comptes-rendus, pièces authentiques états et tableaux concernant les finances de la France depuis 1758 jusqu'en 1787* (Lausanne and Paris, 1788), pp. 32–53.

8. "Mémoire, X^bre [December] 1762," A¹ 3625–43.

under the deceptive rubric of "extraordinary" expenses. During the period of the Seven Years' War the ministry's funds were handled by seven distinct fiscal authorities, each headed by a *trésorier-général.* In addition to the *ordinaire* and *extraordinaire,* there were treasurers of the artillery and engineers, the *Maréchausée,* the *gratifications* or pensions, the Invalides, and the Ecole Militaire.[9]

As was the custom in the eighteenth century, departmental appropriations were drawn not so much from the general pool of receipts as from specific revenues assigned for this purpose. Among the sources of revenue assigned to the ministry of war was the *taillon* or supplementary *taille.* An important part of the ministry's allocation was derived from special assessments made on the *contribuables* for the maintenance of the militia which had been raised. A similar assessment was made for quarters and lodging of the regular army —converted to a cash levy since the troops were in Germany.[10] During wartime the military establishment also benefited from the impositions levied on conquered populations, a practice which will be examined subsequently. The Ecole Militaire, founded in 1751, drew its money from a special tax on playing cards.[11] The *Invalides* and the department of military pensions drew funds from a tax on the appropriations of the *extraordinaire des guerres,* at rates of one denier and three deniers per livre respectively.[12] Choiseul states that the *ordonnancement au comptant* was not used in the ministry of war, and so disbursement usually proceeded as follows: The minister initiated the pay order, which the appropriate treasurer turned over to the recipient; the payee then pre-

9. Frémont, *Payeurs,* I, 56; Mention, *Saint Germain,* p. 9.

10. These two impositions were estimated at 11,816,973 livres for 1759. "Brevet militaire, année 1759," Archives Nationales MSS, Ser. E, Vol. 2374, No. 98.

11. Mention, *Saint Germain,* p. 56.

12. *Ibid.,* p. 242. The *Invalides* enjoyed other special incomes and tax exemptions conferred originally by Louvois. Camille Rousset, *Histoire de Louvois et de son administration politique et militaire* (Paris, 1864), I, 251–53.

sented it to the office of the controller-general, where royal approval was obtained and a fund assigned for payment. The actual payment might take months, depending on the state of the treasury.[13]

In transferring funds to the field, the government avoided sending bullion whenever possible. One method was to utilize the resources of the indispensable court banker. Paris de Montmartel transferred 16,000,000 livres to the army in 1757, using letters of exchange drawn upon the Meinerzhagen brothers, his correspondents in Cologne.[14] Great hopes were placed on the impositions levied in occupied enemy territory, but the yield was always disappointing. To obtain payment the army had to retain control of the area for a considerable period, a condition not always guaranteed by the shifting fortunes of war. Even when the areas were firmly held, it proved extremely difficult to separate the Germans from their money. These levies could be made only in enemy territories, of course, and included not only the ordinary revenues of the dispossessed rulers, but a special *contribution* as well. In 1757 16,000,000 livres were demanded of the Hanoverian and Prussian territories and the Principality of Halberstadt. The sum was due on December 20 of that year, but only a fourth of it had been received the following February when the French were abandoning these areas.[15]

In the field there were three distinct disbursing officers, one for the *extraordinaire des guerres,* one for the artillery, and one for the *contributions;* all three worked under the supervision of the intendant. The army's funds were disbursed to the regiments through the majors, and were composed of numerous separate allocations: the *prêt,* the *masse,* and the *ustensile* were the three major items. The *prêt*

13. Etienne-François, duc de Choiseul, *Mémoires (1719–1785)* (Paris, 1904), pp. 239–41; Frémont, *Payeurs,* I, 51; Dublanchy, *Intendance,* p. 100.
14. "Bordereau des traittes tirées par M. de Montmartel sur Mrs Meinerzhagen de Cologne, ses correspondants" (no date), A² 33–156.
15. "Mémoire sur la situation du service de l'armée du Roi, 12 février 1758," Gayot MSS, 640–193.

was the soldiers' pay, distributed every ten days. The *masse* was a clothing and equipment allotment paid to the captains, about twelve deniers per day for each soldier. The *ustensile* was also paid to the captain; it was to cover expenses of winter quarters and to supplement the insufficient *masse*.[16] Cavalry regiments received an additional allotment for the purpose of purchasing mounts.[17] There were many other minor funds, such as that for purchasing shoes and vests, etc. A very large part of the army's budget was devoted to reimbursing the various companies and *régies* which supplied forage, bread, meat, and other commodities; the policy of assigning specific revenues to cover certain categories of expenses was applied in the field as well as in the central bureaus. The pay of the troops, for example, was to be drawn from the *contributions*.[18]

The lack of funds was perhaps the one problem which most crippled the war effort. The financial difficulties of the old regime were chronic, and war aggravated the situation seriously. In 1757, when war expenses began to mount significantly, the government was already running a deficit and carrying a heavy debt whose service took nearly 20 per cent of the annual revenues. The monarch had borrowed heavily from the tax farmers and was offering 10 per cent interest to hesitant investors in the *rentes viagères*.[19] From this unpromising beginning the government passed very close to bankruptcy, and ended with a crushing postwar debt of nearly 2,000,000,000 livres.[20] The regime put itself in bondage to the court banker, Paris de Montmartel, and his successor, Laborde; but even the financiers could not meet the nation's

16. Bacquet, *Infanterie,* p. 3; Audouin, *Administration,* III, 56.

17. In 1757–1758 this allotment was 1,000 livres per company—hardly a generous amount since a good horse cost 400 livres. "Etat des reparations à faire à une compagnie de cavalerie pendant l'hiver 1757–1758" (no date), A² 56–59.

18. "Mémoire sur la situation du service de l'armée du Roi, 12 février 1758," Gayot MSS, 640–193.

19. Bibliothèque de l'Arsenal, MS 4066A.

20. Carré, *Louis XV,* p. 364.

needs. As the crisis deepened the measures became more desperate. Louis asked for a loan of 30,000,000 from the Spanish monarch, but was refused.[21] In 1760 the monarch sent his silver to the mint and urged his courtiers to do the same.[22] An attempt was even made to float a clandestine loan in England, offering 11.5 per cent.[23]

The ministry of war was the chief victim of the unfortunate state of affairs; by the end of 1760 the department had contracted over 80,000,000 livres in debts.[24] Belle-Isle wrote bitterly: "I spend my life asking for money from the Controller-General, who can give me none." [25] The same deeply pessimistic note recurs constantly in the dispatches from the field. Since no complete budget of field expenses survives, it is impossible to gauge the financial situation there with great accuracy; but a few random references will suffice to illustrate the magnitude of the fiscal crisis. An incomplete financial statement for the Army of the Lower Rhine indicates certain expenses for the year 1758 to have been 14,111,956 livres, of which 4,973,550 were still outstanding.[26] In addition some 3,000,000 livres were yet to be paid to cover expenses of the preceding year.[27] The hospital entrepreneurs had not been reimbursed for their service; one was selling off surplus supplies in order to carry on, while the other was on the point of abandoning operations altogether.[28]

Since the intendant and the treasurers whose work he supervised could not begin to cover current expenses with

21. "Jean Josephe de Laborde," *Biographie universelle*, XXII, 287.

22. Barbier, *Journal*, VII, 200.

23. Mouffle d'Angerville, *Louis XV*, III, 144.

24. Choiseul's "Mémoire, X^bre [December], 1762," A¹ 3625–43; Belle-Isle to Contades, Sept. 8, 1759, A¹ 3522–122.

25. Belle-Isle to Contades, July 26, 1758, A¹ 3479–245.

26. "Etat général et sommaire, dépenses extraordinaires, 13 janvier 1759," Gayot MSS, 651–113.

27. Belle-Isle to Clermont, May 6, 1758, A¹ 3475–79.

28. Gayot to Belle-Isle, Dec. 13, 1758, Gayot MSS, 650–179; Crémilles to Gayot, Nov. 2, 1758, Gayot MSS, 650–10. The entrepreneurs for the stationary hospitals were forced into bankruptcy in 1760, chiefly because the government had paid only a fraction of what it owed them. Mention, *Saint Germain*, Introduction, p. xxi.

their limited resources, they used a variety of expedients. The less vociferous creditors found that the funds assigned to them had been given to someone else, and the manipulations of this nature made the army's finances an impenetrable maze.[29] The soldiers' pay was sometimes made in foreign currency, though the troops grumbled much over this.[30] Many accounts were settled by the issuance of *billets de caisse,* negotiable promissory notes. Because of the government's shaky credit, however, these were discounted at 20 or 30 per cent even in the early months of the war.[31]

The payment of soldiers' salaries or the *prêt* was considered a sacred obligation which was to be met scrupulously, whatever the sacrifice. At all times funds were to be on hand for a month's expenditures in this connection, but this was seldom the case. At times the pay was assured for no more than eight days; [32] there are several examples of destitute regiments which contracted loans from private individuals in order to pay their troops.[33] Officers' salaries were paid with even greater irregularity. In 1760 the pay of the general officers was two or three years in arrears.[34]

The financial embarrassment of the field army was much increased by widespread malversation and corruption. The money that the army might have obtained from the conquered populations was often collected by general officers for their own purposes. Marshal Richelieu set the pace in 1757 by selling "safeguards" to enemy towns and pocketing the proceeds; the magnificent town house which he built in Paris after his recall was dubbed the "Hanover Pavilion" by a

29. In 1758 the *subsistence* fund was "raided" for some 900,000 livres in this manner. Belle-Isle to Gayot, Dec. 22, 1758, Gayot MSS, 651–93.

30. In this regard, see Paulmy's letter to Gayot of Dec. 27, 1757, Gayot MSS, 639–57.

31. Richelieu to Paris Duverney, July 27, 1757, *Correspondance Richelieu–Paris Duverney,* I, 67.

32. Bourcet, *Mémoires,* I, 236.

33. See for example the case of the garrison at Liege, mentioned in Belle-Isle's letter to Gayot of Dec. 16, 1758, Gayot MSS, 651–159.

34. Mention, *Saint Germain,* Introduction, p. xviii.

knowing public.[35] Following Richelieu's example officers who commanded garrisons in occupied towns demanded a lavish maintenance at the expense of the population.[36] Contades was still struggling unsuccessfully to stamp out the practice in 1759.[37] The army's meager treasury was depleted further by extravagant gifts to general officers. Clermont, with a monthly salary of 5,000 livres was authorized by Louis to take 14,000 livres from the army's funds, but to conceal the gift under the rubric of extraordinary expenses "by which means neither the Treasurer of the Army, nor the Controller-General, nor anyone else will know it." [38]

Outright fraud was no less common. While the general officers were given lavish emoluments the lesser grades were very poorly paid and were driven to fraud by necessity.[39] Much theft and misappropriation went undiscovered, but occasionally there were spectacular scandals. The treasurer of the Army of the Lower Rhine in 1757 had an ingenious system. He collected specie in Cologne upon presentation of Montmartel's letters of exchange. He then had it reminted, using a heavy admixture of base metal. It was estimated that in this way he gained about three million livres.[40] Even more colossal thefts were perpetrated by contractors. The *munitionnaire* who supplied bread to the small contingent in Canada stole some six million livres.[41]

35. Duclos, *Mémoires,* II, 287; Barbier, *Journal,* VII, 58.

36. For some instances of this practice, see Rousset, *Gisors,* pp. 346–48.

37. Contades to Belle-Isle, June 7, 1759, A¹ 3517–77. Not all of the garrison commanders made such lavish demands on their hosts. The commander at Frankfort who was quartered in the home of the young Goethe carefully refrained from nailing his maps to the walls. Johann Wolfgang Goethe, *Aus meinem Leben: Dichtung und Wahrheit* (Vol. X of *Gedenkausgabe der Werke, Briefe und Gespräche* [Zurich, 1948]), p. 96.

38. Belle-Isle to Clermont, June 9, 1758, A² 38–26. In a similar form of deception Belle-Isle urged the generals to paint the financial situation in the darkest colors: "Car malheureusement on ne peut pas agir avec la franchise que j'aime. . . ." Belle-Isle to Soubise, Feb. 6, 1759, A¹ 3512–27.

39. The monthly salary of a French infantry captain was only ninety-five livres, as against one hundred and ninety-one for his Prussian counterpart. Further comparative figures are to be found in Dussauge, *Etudes,* p. 292.

40. "Affaire du Sr. Mauvillain, Trésorier de l'armée des Maréchaux d'Estrées et de Richelieu" (no date), A² 33–145.

41. Audouin, *Administration,* III, 185–86.

The question arises as to how well France used her financial resources in comparison to the other belligerents. Saint Germain, who knew the military establishment intimately, insisted that the French king spent proportionately much more than the other monarchs for his army, but that they were no better salaried, equipped, or supplied;[42] Guibert, who examined military accounts, stated that the French spent two or perhaps three times as much as the other belligerents.[43] Guibert's calculations, which relate only to the postwar establishment, show France as maintaining 140,000 men with 106,000,000 livres. Prussia was expending 56,000,000 livres on 180,000 soldiers, while Austria maintained about the same number of men with a budget of 62,000,000 livres.[44] Guibert insisted that the same disparity existed during war, but any calculations are rendered difficult by lack of accurate knowledge of the French budget. Assuming that the figure was in the neighborhood of 200,000,000 livres for 400,000 men, including household troops and militia, the cost per soldier would be about 500 livres annually. Frederick maintained an average force of 270,000 men on a war budget of 15,000,000 thalers or 82,000,000 livres,[45] thus each Prussian soldier would have cost about 300 livres annually. Open to question as such figures are, they do seem to bear out Guibert's assertion.[46]

Some of the reasons for the high French war costs have already been noted. The proliferation of officers was certainly one serious disadvantage.[47] The widespread use of the wasteful and obsolescent contract system for supplies was another factor, and more will be said of this subsequently.

---

42. "Mémoire sur les vices du militaire francais," *Correspondance Saint Germain–Paris Duverney,* I, 197.
43. *Guerre moderne,* IV, 252.
44. *Ibid.,* p. 251.
45. The figure given in Delbrück, *Kriegskunst,* IV, 337, n. 2.
46. Whitworth estimates that the English soldier cost approximately sixty-six pounds, and the Hanoverian twenty-five pounds, but unfortunately he does not explain how he arrived at these figures. See his *Ligonier,* p. 246.
47. In 1789 officers' pay consumed more than half the military budget. Jules Michelet, *Histoire de la Révolution Française* (Pléiade edition), I, 123.

Moreover, the French learned to their sorrow that for those who have no money the cost is always much higher. France's enemies were in the enviable position of being better able to pay cash for their needs. Frederick started the war with a full treasury and could rely upon an annual subsidy of 670,000 English pounds. Ferdinand's army was also better financed; its meticulously balanced accounts speak eloquently of its superiority in this regard.[48] By contrast, the French were obliged to rely upon an already overstrained credit and issue great quantities of discredited paper. The failure to have a fund on hand for anticipated expenses meant that the army could not buy up stocks of forage in the summer months when the price was lower, and so it was obliged to fill these needs only as they arose, paying perhaps double in the process.[49] Multiplied many times over, this disadvantage goes a long way toward explaining the exorbitant cost of the war for a regime that would collapse in bankruptcy a scant three decades later.

48. The annual budgets for 1759, 1760, and 1761 appear in Westphalen, *Feldzüge,* I, 1114–23.

49. See in this connection Belle-Isle's revealing letter to Contades of Sept. 20, 1759, A¹ 3522–154.

9

Supply and Equipment

In war as in peace the old regime turned to private enterprise to fulfil many vital functions; the Farmers General had their military counterparts in the various concerns who supplied the armies with their everyday needs. These entrepreneurs established elaborate organizations with headquarters in Paris and numerous agents with the armies. They mobilized enormous amounts of capital and matériel, and administered a large bureaucracy; they were in fact "shadow" ministries, charged with a significant part of the war effort.

The *munitionnaires* serve admirably to illustrate the importance of such enterprises. The *munitionnaires* contracted to supply bread to the entire military establishment. The agreement stipulated the daily ration at twenty-four ounces, composed of two-thirds wheat and one-third rye, for which the *munitionnaire* would receive thirty-three deniers per ration.[1] This gigantic concern fed 280,000 men for six years, had thousands of workers, great numbers of wagons, and used 23,000 horses.[2] Its annual budget ran to 20,000,000 livres.[3]

While the *munitionnaires* fed all of the armies, other supplies were provided by contractors for each force. The Army of the Lower Rhine was supplied with meat by a concern which was similar in organization to that of the *munitionnaires*. It distributed a *quarteron* or quarter pound of meat to each soldier as his daily ration. Traditionally the distribution

1. "Mémoire historique des vivres de Flandres et d'Allemagne de guerre de 157 à 1762 inclus," "Mémoires historiques," 230–6. (Since this manuscript comprises all of volume 230, it has standard pagination.)
2. *Ibid.*, p. 2.
3. *Ibid.*, p. 4.

was made only during the campaign months, but during the war meat rations were accorded to troops in winter quarters as well.[4]

No entrepreneur could be enticed into accepting the task of supplying forage to the army, and so this service was performed by a *régie*. This government corporation also had numerous personnel; the perishable nature and the bulk of the commodity it supplied required it to maintain great storehouses or *magasins* in France and Germany. The daily ration for the cavalry was twelve pounds of hay and two-thirds of a *boisseau* of oats; the infantry ration was slightly smaller.[5]

Apparently these organizations relied primarily on France as a source of supply, though every effort was made to obtain these commodities in Germany. The resources of the French border provinces were most used so as to minimize the costs of transportation. The *munitionnaires'* memoir previously cited states that the bulk of its flour and grain was drawn from the frontier provinces.[6] In 1759 4,000,000 rations of forage were called for in Soissons, Flandre, Champagne, Metz, Alsace, and Hainaut—a quantity sufficient to carry an army through six months of winter quarters.[7]

In enemy territories it was possible to raise additional supplies by means of impositions, similar to the levies of money. In allied and neutral territories supplies could be obtained by requisitions or *lettres requisitoriales*. This system had originally been devised for the use of Austrian troops, and at Vienna's suggestion the German states accorded the same privilege to the French in their legal status as auxiliaries to Austria. The intendant instituted the request, which was then presented to the German authorities by the French diplomatic

4. "Fournitures aux troupes de l'Armée du Roy en Allemagne" (no date) A² 35–50. Unfortunately the contract of the meat suppliers was not found in the course of research.

5. "Mémoire, Quartier d'Hiver 1758–1759," Gayot MSS, 653–2.

6. "Mémoires historiques," 230–32.

7. The *arrêts* ordering these rations are to be found in Archives Nationales, Ser. E, Vol. 2680, Nos. 17, 59, 60, 68, 73, and 127.

representative. The authorities thereupon took measures to fill the order, and were paid for what they supplied according to a fixed scale of prices. It appears that these purchases were made both for the entrepreneurs and for the army directly.[8]

The court much favored this system of impositions and requisitions, since the cost was low and the resources of the realm were not depleted. Unfortunately there were enormous problems involved. The French became inextricably entangled in the chaotic political organization of the German states, particularly in the matter of enclaves. The County of Hanau was a Prussian dependency, but when contributions were levied here, the yield was always very meager; certain territories in the dependency were exempt because they belonged to the Grand Master of the Teutonic Order.[9] Charitable institutions of Frankfort and the Order of Malta also owned extensive properties in Hanau, and their outcry further hindered the collection of supplies.[10]

Allied and neutral princes were not eager to raise supplies for the French, knowing that their reimbursement would be less than certain. The procedure was for the army to issue receipts and to promise suppliers that the government would make payment "as soon as finances will permit." [11] These assurances were discounted heavily, and many authorities refused to deliver supplies unless paid in specie. One forage officer had to surrender his watch in order to get a delivery of desperately needed forage.[12]

The supplies from the above sources could be supplemented by passing *marchés* or contracts with German entrepreneurs for the delivery of items otherwise unobtainable.

8. The procedure for requisition is fully explained in Bernis' letter to Paulmy of Jan. 6, 1758, A² 56–83.

9. Belle-Isle to Bernis, March 26, 1758, A¹ 3508–149.

10. Comte de Lorges to Belle-Isle, March 27, 1758, A¹ 3508–151; "Mémoire du Bourgemestre et des Magistrats de la Ville Impériale de Francfort sur la Main, 15 mars 1758," A¹ 3508–125.

11. Belle-Isle to Soubise, Jan. 4, 1759, A¹ 3511–30.

12. Comte de Lorges to Crémilles, April 9, 1758, A¹ 3474–79.

When the normal means of purchase failed, as they often did, the field commander insisted that the *marché* be used and compelled the intendant to take this action. The intendant was "between the hammer and the anvil," [13] since the ministry strongly disapproved. "The idea of entrepreneurs is false," intoned Paris Duverney, "since it is impossible to execute and ruinous. The supplies are either in the occupied areas or they are not. If they are not, where are the entrepreneurs who can furnish them?" [14] Nor would the "Flour Bag General" give credence to the harrowing reports of shortages which came from the armies: "I do not believe I am in error, *Monseigneur*, in thinking that you cannot lack for subsistence. I have the relevant figures before me, and these figures are more reliable than all the reasoning in the world." [15]

The court's objections to the *marché* were primarily the increased cost of supplies received through this medium. The "official" price of a ration of forage in the requisition system was sixteen sous, but contractors charged from twenty-one to twenty-five sous.[16] Sheer necessity led the intendant to ignore the injunctions of Versailles, and constant use was made of the *marché*.[17] The ministry found little comfort in the assurances that "the Jews who handle this enterprise have as good a reputation as Jews can have." [18]

Before attempting to assess the efficiency and success of the French supply system, it is only fair to say something of the enormity of the logistical problems posed in eighteenth-

---

13. M. Bellombre to M. du Pont, April 20, 1758, A² 58–38.

14. Paris Duverney to Richelieu, Aug. 18, 1757, *Correspondance Richelieu–Paris Duverney*, I, 93.

15. Paris Duverney to Richelieu, Aug. 14, 1757, *ibid.*, p. 80.

16. "Etat des Fournitures, Armée du Bas Rhin" (no date), Gayot MSS, 642–107.

17. In the months of March through July, 1758, alone, the Intendant of the Army of the Lower Rhine negotiated no fewer than twenty-seven contracts for hay, oats, straw, wood, and sacks for a total sum of 2,394,623 livres. "Etat des marchés faits pour assurer la subsistance des troupes en fourages pendant les mois de mars, avril, mai, juin et juillet 1758," Gayot MSS, 644–179.

18. Clermont to Belle-Isle, April 18, 1758, A¹ 3474–154.

century warfare. In truth criticism tends to pale when one considers that the army was drawing much of its needs from a distance of several hundred miles with a very unsatisfactory transportation system, and that much of this transportation took place in the winter months, with all the additional hazards of that season. The large number of effectives in Germany—as many as 200,000—required tremendous amounts of provisions and matériel of all kinds. In addition, for every two soldiers there was a non-combatant who likewise had to be maintained.[19] The lavish rations of food and forage accorded to the general officers placed further demands on the supply system. Concerning these last two commodities, some figures can be cited to show the enormous quantities required. According to the calculations of Audouin an army of 100,000 men consumed 200,000 pounds of flour each day.[20] The 75,000 horses used in Germany required during the winter months a total of 8,818,636 forage rations—some 70,000 tons of hay and 4,000,000 bushels of oats.[21]

Customarily the bread ration was issued every four days, the bread being edible for about nine days after baking. The rations were delivered to the army by convoys. The field ovens were generally placed about three days' march from the grain stores and two days' march from the army.[22] It must be said to the credit of the *munitionnaire* that the bread supply never failed disastrously in the Army of the Lower Rhine. It should be added, however, that time and time

---

19. Bacquet, *Infanterie*, p. 50.
20. *Administration*, III, 76.
21. "Mémoire sur la subsistance en fourrages de l'armée d'Allemagne pendant le quartier d'hiver de 1759 à 1760" (no date), A¹ 3523–18. For the consumption of other commodities, see "Etat des differents denrées nécessaires pour l'approvisionnement de bouche pour 6 mois pour une garnison de dix mille hommes," Nov. 26, 1758, A¹ 3506–368.
22. Delbrück, *Kriegskunst*, IV, 344; Dussauge, *Etudes*, p. 211. Much information can be found in Louis Dupré d'Aulnay, *Traité général des subsistances militaires qui comprend la fourniture du pain de munition, des fourages & de la viande aux armées et aux troupes de garnisons; ensemble celle des hôpitaux & des équipages des vivres & de l'artillerie, par marché ou résultat du Conseil, à forfait ou par régie* (Paris, 1744).

again troop movements were canceled for the very purpose
of preventing such a failure. This can be seen quite clearly
during the summer of 1759. Contades wrote from Corbach
on June 10 that he had planned to advance but that the ovens
at Corbach from which the bread was to be drawn would not
be ready for some two weeks, because of the lack of materials.[23] Two days later he reported that the army would remain in Corbach for the distribution of June 13, drawing
from the ovens at Marburg; the *munitionnaire* promised,
however, to supply the army at a distance of eight leagues
from Corbach, still drawing on the installation at Marburg.[24]
On June 15 Contades had advanced to Meerhoff, but could
go no further. The Corbach ovens would be completed by
June 24, and the first rations from this installation could be
drawn on June 28, after which the army would advance
again.[25] By now there were new problems, for more ovens
had to be built at Cassel and Paderborn, and the *munitionnaire* believed he would be able to supply the army eighteen
leagues beyond Paderborn—providing the ovens could be put
into operation by July 6.[26] The army continued to creep
forward in this manner, "leap-frogging" from one set of
ovens to another, until it encountered the enemy at Minden.
The engagement presented the *munitionnaire* with an even
greater dilemma. He had to make dispositions in the event
of a victory and continued advance, and also to try to guess
the probable line of retreat if the French were defeated. As
it turned out, Contades hastily retired some thirty-five
leagues, using an entirely different route from that used for
the advance. Fortunately the representative of the *munitionnaire* was the very able Marquet de Peyre, who successfully
anticipated the retrograde movement and managed to keep

---

23. Contades to Belle-Isle, June 10, 1759, A¹ 3517–130.
24. Contades to Belle-Isle, June 12, 1759, A¹ 3517–155.
25. Contades to Belle-Isle, June 15, 1759, A¹ 3517–198.
26. Contades to Belle-Isle, June 20, 1759, A¹ 3517–298.

the army supplied.[27] The meat and forage supplies, however, failed almost completely, and the troops committed heavy depredations. The outraged peasants in turn attacked the wagonloads of wounded, and several villages were put to the torch by the French.[28]

Of all supply problems that of forage was the most crucial and the most difficult to solve. For approximately half of the year, from October to June, the army used *fourrage sec*—hay and oats. For the rest of the year the horses were to be maintained as much as possible on *fourrage vert*. The winter months were the really critical ones, and the harassed minister wrote: "You can rest assured that I go to bed thinking about forage and get up again still thinking about it." [29] The distribution problems were somewhat different from those of the *munitionnaire*. Since the period of dry forage coincided with that of winter quarters the army was at least stationary. Numerous depots were established at the beginning of the winter to serve the various cantonments. Elaborate and sometimes desperate measures were taken to reduce the winter consumption. In 1758–1759, 20,000 horses were brought back to winter in France, the army being thereby deprived of much of its mobility.[30] Six cavalry regiments were also recalled to France.[31] The most stringent directives were issued to prohibit the use of dry forage during the summer months— a practice that was notoriously widespread among higher officers.[32] The system of the *rachat* permitted officers to sell their unused forage rations back to the *régie* for sixteen sous,

27. His careful dispositions are explained in a letter of his brother, Marquet de Bourgade, to Belle-Isle, Aug. 11, 1759, A¹ 3520–152.

28. Mercoyrol de Beaulieu, *Campagnes,* p. 239.

29. Belle-Isle to Contades, Nov. 6, 1758, A¹ 3486–79.

30. Belle-Isle to M. Durand d'Aubigny, Nov. 23, 1758, Gayot MSS, 650–257. The *munitionnaires* brought back to France all but a bare minimum of 1,600 horses. Contades to Belle-Isle, Nov. 21, 1758, A¹ 3487–65.

31. Belle-Isle to Durand d'Aubigny, Jan. 20, 1759, A¹ 3542–109.

32. See in this connection Belle-Isle's irate letter to Contades of July 26, 1758, A¹ 3479–245.

and in practice they were given as much as twenty-one sous per ration.[33] Despite these measures there was almost always a serious shortage. The official ration was to contain sixteen pounds of hay, but early in 1758 the hay ration was cut to twelve pounds, the deficiency being made up with ten pounds of straw.[34] In the winter of 1758–1759 the ration dropped as low as ten pounds;[35] in the following winter it fell to six.[36] Sometimes the supply failed altogether; when Saint Germain made his forced march to join Broglie at the battle of Corbach in 1760 he had no choice but to leave his artillery behind, the artillery horses having had no forage for nearly a week.[37]

In the summer months the army relied chiefly on green fodder supplied by forage parties, a system that is best described in the words of a contemporary:

> The command of a general forage required military dispositions, posts, advantageous locations surrounded by a chain of troops to protect the foragers. These latter then left camp in several columns, and when they had arrived at the designated places, the foragers were turned loose to dash off with frightful disorder, ravaging the fields, marking with their sabers the areas they had chosen—always far beyond their needs; forming enormous bundles too heavy for their horses, then choosing their routes haphazardly, encumbering the roads and arriving in the camp in the middle of the night with horses so exhausted that the forage could not restore them. . . .[38]

The problems of obtaining green forage were always in evidence. Military necessity sometimes dictated movement through areas that had already been denuded by the passage

33. Castelnau to De Gaix, Jan. 16, 1759, *Lettres*, p. 91.
34. "Lettre circulaire de S.A.S. le comte de Clermont," April 20, 1758, A¹ 3501–298.
35. Letter of M. Feydeau de Saint Christophe to his father, Dec. 30, 1758, P. J. F. Feydeau de Saint Christophe, *Correspondance inédite relative à la Guerre de Sept Ans et à la Guerre de l'Indépendance Américaine* (Paris, 1921), p. 31.
36. Feydeau de Saint Christophe to M. de Chavagnac, Dec. 3, 1759, *ibid.*, p. 34.
37. Mention, *Saint Germain*, Introduction, p. xxvi.
38. Ray, *Réflexions*, p. 170.

of hostile or friendly foragers. The army's enormous needs soon siphoned off the produce of even the richest areas, and then the commander had no choice but to change position. Often forage had to be obtained at great distance; in October, 1759, the Army of the Lower Rhine was drawing on districts thirteen leagues away, and the forage parties were spending twelve hours on the road.[39]

The official correspondence reveals that great quantities of supplies were lost through waste or spoilage. In part the losses resulted from the hazards of war, particularly a hasty retreat. There is strong evidence, however, of palpable negligence. In September, 1758, out of 7,317 bales of hay ordered from Metz, only 2,255 bales arrived, and half of these were so rotten they had to be thrown into the Rhine.[40] Two million rations of forage were lost at Wesel because of improper storage.[41] Much of the loss can also be attributed to bad logistical planning. In the winter of 1757–1758 the garrison at Hameln was ordered to draw its forage and firewood from a distance of thirty leagues, while there were abundant supplies at hand reserved for another garrison.[42] During the same winter the army was storing quantities of locally obtained grain in the more exposed forward areas and drawing on supplies from the rear for its everyday needs. When the army was obliged to retreat the laboriously collected grain had to be destroyed.[43]

The unending scandals in the supply system testify to the prevalence of malversation and fraud, especially in the chaotic forage *régie*. Warehouse keepers would sell their stocks in secret and then attribute the discrepancy in their accounts to spoilage.[44] The minister was well aware of these practices;

39. Castelnau to De Gaix, Oct. 12, 1759, *Lettres,* p. 124.
40. "Etat des envoyes en foin," Sept. 24, 1758, Gayot MSS, 648–38.
41. Observations of Gayot, Feb. 10, 1758, Gayot MSS, 640–110.
42. Broglie to Richelieu, Jan. 25, 1758, A^1 3471–169.
43. Guibert, *Tactique,* II, 297–98.
44. Memoir of M. Surlaville, 1758, as cited in Mention, *Saint Germain,* pp. 223–24.

he instructed the intendant not to multiply the number of warehouses unnecessarily, "in order not to multiply the abuses which ordinarily attend their exploitation." [45] The mismanagement and corruption of the forage *régie* reached a peak in 1758, when the *régisseur* himself absconded.[46]

Most of the shortcomings in the supply services can be traced to the contract system. The entrepreneurs escaped effective control by the intendant; their compliance was difficult to obtain since their liability was limited. Frequently they had powerful connections at court. Their margin of profit lay between the quality of service they rendered and the remuneration they received. "Their gains are less considerable," wrote Guibert, "to the degree that they are less avid, more honest, more exact in their service." [47] The majority of them were considered "a league of bloodsuckers." [48] The only exception were the *munitionnaires,* whose service was much praised. Guibert, who examined their accounts, stated that their profit was only "legitimate gain." [49]

All of the belligerents encountered serious difficulties in keeping their armies fed, as any history of the conflict will show; but the French seem to have been at a distinct disadvantage, particularly as opposed to their enemy in Germany. With a smaller army Ferdinand's needs were less. He was usually operating in territories whose inhabitants were favorable to him and readily lent assistance. His requisition system was more equitable, and what he took he could pay for in gold.[50] Plentiful funds also permitted him to purchase supplies in the neutral Netherlands.[51] The French themselves made an unfavorable comparison between the situation of

45. Belle-Isle to Gayot, March 26, 1758, Gayot MSS, 641–216.
46. "Affaire de Millin de Grandmaison régisseur des fourages pendant la campagne de 1757 et au commencement de celle de 1758" (no date), A² 36–4.
47. *Tactique,* II, 269.
48. Audouin, *Administration,* III, 29.
49. *Tactique,* II, 267.
50. Westphalen, *Feldzüge,* I, 114.
51. Early in 1758 he spent 100,000 pounds for the purchase of Dutch grain. Ferdinand to Frederick, April 3, 1758, *ibid.,* II, 322.

their army and that of the enemy; French commanders were often lectured on this matter. It was very unfortunate, Belle-Isle wrote to Clermont, that the Army of the Lower Rhine could not find provisions "while Prince Ferdinand can subsist anywhere." [52]

The most serious charge that can be leveled at the French was that their system of supply was obsolescent. Most of the belligerents had made substantial progress in concentrating the logistical functions in the hands of competent governmental authorities, usually following the pattern of Frederick and his famed Directorium.[53] In the Prussian service officers did not regard matters of supply as beneath them. Frederick's *Intendant der Armee* was Colonel von Arnstedt, in whose province lay *étapes,* provisions, and bakeries. Generalmajor von Massow was responsible for clothing, arms, and remounts. Each Prussian *corps d'armée* had its *Feldkriegskommissariat.*[54] Ligonier militarized the English commissariat along Prussian lines in 1760.[55] Though the Russian army still obtained its supplies through a mixed system of military and private agencies, it had a General War Commissariat and a "provisionmaster" as well.[56] Even Austria, whose military establishment was despised by the French, had made significant progress in this field. Thanks to the reforms of the 1750's, Maria Theresa's army entered the conflict with a new system in which provisions and supply were placed in the hands of governmental boards.[57] France was the only

---

52. Belle-Isle to Clermont, June 22, 1758, A¹ 3477–50.

53. For a brief survey of the supply systems of the belligerents in this period, particularly that of Prussia, see Bernard von Baumann, *Studien über die Verpflegung der Kriegsheere im Felde* (Leipzig and Heidelburg, 1867–74), I, 281–85. Oberstleutnant Otto Meixner, *Historischer Rückblick auf die Verpflegung der Armeen im Felde: Lieferung I* (Vienna, 1895), contains some general observations on the period.

54. Curt Jany, *Geschichte der Königlich-Preussischen Armee bis zum Jehre 1807* (Berlin, 1928–1929), II, 209–10.

55. Whitworth, *Ligonier,* p. 324.

56. L. G. Beskrovnii, *Russkaia Armiia i Flot v XVIII veke* (Moscow, 1958), pp. 120–24.

57. Johann Mailath, *Geschichte von Östreich* (Hamburg, 1850), V, 52; Hugo Hantsch, *Die Geschichte Österreichs, 1648–1918* (Vienna, 1947), p. 164.

major belligerent which had not established a commissariat of some form.

The reasons for the French adherence to traditional methods of provisioning are several. First of all, the innate conservatism of the military establishment was hostile to army reforms. After all, as Paris Duverney pointed out, had not the generals of Louis XIV executed the greatest deeds with the very same system? [58] This attitude was widespread, though sporadically the government attempted minor improvements. Thus quantities of a mysterious "nutritive powder" were shipped to the army. Six ounces of this unknown compound were reputed to be equivalent to a daily ration of bread, but it seems to have been an indifferent success, since there is little reference to it.[59] By contrast the government ignored far more important innovations in supply methods. The outstanding case was that of the field ovens. The Austrian and Prussian armies had adopted portable iron field ovens which seem to have been very successful. The French military attaché in Vienna offered to send plans of the Austrian model, but the proposal elicited no interest at Versailles.[60] The French forces continued to have their bread baked in brick ovens, a practice that was slow and costly. To supply a hundred thousand men some forty ovens were needed; often materials were in such short supply that houses

58. "Mémoire particulière de M. Paris Duverney pour S.A.S. le comte de Clermont, 25 janvier 1758," A² 36–37.

59. "Manière de se servir de la poudre nourissante," May, 1758, Gayot MSS, 642–290. The Prussians experimented with a similar powder, with the same disappointing results. Jany, *Geschichte*, II, 216. The chief purpose in both cases was to free the army from its dependence upon bread convoys and bakeries. Though biscuit or "hardtack" was known and used in exceptional cases, it was never regarded as an adequate substitute. Apparently the medical profession felt it could not sustain the soldiers. Colombier, *Code*, I, 159.

60. M. de Marainville to Belle-Isle, June 2, 1759, A¹ 3517–15. Lack of funds may have been part of the reason for failing to adopt portable ovens. According to Audouin, D'Argenson experimented with them before he left the ministry; the idea was later dropped because the ovens cost 2,400 livres each and it was easier to pay brickmasons little by little. *Administration,* III, 77–78.

had to be demolished to obtain the brick, and the installations required as much as two weeks to build.[61]

The tactical consequences of this state of affairs were far-reaching. Of all commodities supplied to the army, bread was the most critical. Horses might do without forage, men might march without pay or shoes, but the bread and flour convoys were like a gigantic umbilical cord which kept the army within five days' march of its source of supply. Profiting in part from new techniques, Frederick was often able to increase the logistical "reach" of his armies to seven, nine, and ten days' march, with results that can well be imagined.[62]

One suspects that the *munitionnaires* may have been instrumental in preserving the old system; in any event they objected to increasing the size of the loaf to correspond with the twenty-eight ounce bread ration issued after 1758; the loaf continued to be twenty-four ounces because "the bakers would have too much difficulty in breaking the habit of preparing bread in this form." [63]

It is quite probable that the government would have been unable to abandon the outmoded entrepreneurial system even if it had desired to do so. The entrepreneurs were men of wealth and power whose interests would have been difficult to attack.[64] Even more important, the contract system enabled the government to obtain credit by compensating the entrepreneurs lavishly but gradually. These concerns were also called upon to take a considerable amount of government paper. The *munitionnaires* alone accepted 39,000,000 livres in this manner, taking a loss of from 30 to 60 per cent. In 1763 the government still owed the company 15,512,726 livres.[65] Considering the government's desperate financial straits it seems probable, as Guibert remarked, that the

61. Guibert, *Tactique,* II, 283; Belle-Isle to Contades, June 16, 1759, A¹ 3517–201.

62. Baumann, *Verpflegung,* I, 285.

63. Belle-Isle to Gayot, May 13, 1758, A¹ 3502–161.

64. For Saint Germain's bitter struggle with the *munitionnaires* during his ministry, see his *Mémoires,* pp. 28–31.

65. "Mémoires historiques," 230–156.

entrepreneurial system was one of "usury lending to necessity." [66]

In general the army's matériel and equipment were supplied through the military authorities rather than private concerns. For this reason these services escaped most of the abuses of the contract system. One exception, however, was the soldier's uniform, part of which was supplied by the captain. The government provided the soldier's shirts, shoes, trousers, and hat, and the captain was to supply the rest with funds from the *masse*.[67] Although regulations stipulated the quality of cloth to be used, the government did not exercise effective control over the captain's purchases.[68] The contracts which the captains negotiated for the needs of their companies had to be submitted for approval, but this was no obstacle to the cupidity of the company officers. They simply agreed with unscrupulous merchants to negotiate two contracts—one to satisfy the authorities and another for the actual purchase. The second of these would call for inferior materials or a smaller quantity and a rebate to the captain.[69]

Clothing and equipment were not supplied continuously but generally during the period of winter quarters, when the regiments could dedicate themselves to *réparations*. As soon as the units entered their cantonments an inventory was taken of each company's needs and the orders placed.[70]

66. *Tactique,* II, 302.

67. In 1754 the cost of the soldier's clothing and equipment was estimated at 79 livres, 10 sous. Babeau, *Soldats,* p. 107. The uniform was as unsuitable as it was expensive; indeed, it is hard to imagine any clothing less appropriate for campaigning than the dress of the eighteenth-century soldier. Guibert, Saxe, Saint Germain, and others railed against the tight fitting coats, the many-buttoned gaiters, and the frivolous headgear; yet the uniform changed little. Its chief appeal, apparently, was an aesthetic one. Officers wanted their soldiers to be fashionably dressed for the same reason that they preferred men with handsome faces and well-turned calves. The term *joli soldat* was much used.

68. *Ibid.,* p. 109.

69. The ministry was well aware of such practices. See D'Argenson's notes on Captain B——, reproduced in Tuetey, *Officiers,* p. 340.

70. See, for example, "Etat des Réparations à faire à une compagnie de Cavalerie pendant l'hiver 1757–1758" (no date), A² 56–69.

Eventually the *ballots* or consignments of matériel were collected and sent to their destinations. Usually these *réparations* were not completed when the next campaign opened. There were frequent complaints of the slowness of shipments. After two months in winter quarters Contades wrote: "The army is completely naked, no regiment has received any of its supplies, all the infantry is without tents, and the same is true of the cavalry. Most of the horses have neither saddles nor bits, and the artillery repairs, both for the park and the regiments, have barely begun." [71] Another general lamented: "The French armies, which during the preceding wars were always ready to enter into campaign in the month of April, become more cumbersome every year. . . ." [72] The chief cause of this lack of preparation most likely lay in the changing nature of warfare. Guibert, one of the more acute observers, put his finger on the basic problem: "The campaigns have become longer; the custom of using winter quarters is scarcely observed any more; hence the needs have doubled, the replacements are continual, nothing can be repaired save with haste and enormous expense." [73] There is much evidence to support this thesis. From April, 1757, to November, 1758, the Army of the Lower Rhine had only twelve weeks of repose, and was driven from its winter quarters twice, once in the middle of the winter. By the summer of 1758 it was in a pitiable state. The infantry had neither tents nor cooking gear, and three thousand cavalry horses were sent to the rear because there were no saddles or bridles for them. [74]

The field of armaments was one in which the states of early modern Europe had long been active. By the eighteenth century the role of the state was a preponderant one; most

71. "Copie de la lettre écrite par M. le M^{al} de Contades à M. le M^{al} de Soubise le 2 janvier 1759," A^1 3511-5 *bis*.
72. Chevalier de Muy to Belle-Isle, May 22, 1759, A^1 3516–104.
73. *Guerre moderne,* IV, 250.
74. Clermont to Belle-Isle, June 3, 1758, A^1 3476–86; Mortaigne to Belle-Isle, June 11, 1758, A^1 3490–49.

governments were already wrestling with the modern problems of obsolescence and the stockpiling of strategic materials. Artillery underwent continuous development in the period. While the smoothbore flintlock musket remained the standard arm of the infantry, it was steadily being perfected. In France alone, four successive models were introduced: those of 1717, 1754, 1763, and 1777.[75]

The system of arms procurement used in France during the Seven Years' War dated from the late seventeenth century and was the method used by most belligerents. The state still did not manufacture its own weapons, strictly speaking. Production of small arms was confided to the *Manufactures Royales;* in essence these were groups of entrepreneurs in various arms centers who worked exclusively for the government. The most important of these in the eighteenth century were located in Charleville and Saint Etienne. The *armes blanches*—sabres and bayonets—produced at Klingenthal, and the cannon cast in various foundries fell under a similar regime.

The entrepreneurs at Charleville and Saint Etienne engaged themselves to supply quotas of muskets at a price set by contract, and of a quality acceptable to the government. Royal inspectors, usually artillery officers, watched each step of manufacture and tested the arms before their acceptance. The entrepreneurs copied arsenal models and adhered to specifications set by the artillery.[76]

Available evidence indicates that the French armies were well supplied with small arms of domestic manufacture and did not have to resort to importation, an advantage other

75. There is no general work on armament production in the old regime. For small arms manufacture the best printed sources are monographs: L.-J. Gras, *Historique de l'armurerie stéphanoise* (Saint Etienne, 1905); Henri Manceau, *La manufacture d'armes de Charleville* (Charleville, 1962). For the artillery, see Colonel E. Picard and Lieutenant R. Jouan, *L'artillerie française aux XVIIIᵉ siècle* (Paris, 1906).

76. For a good account of relations between small arms entrepreneurs and the government, see Gras, *Armurerie*, pp. 25–64.

belligerents did not always enjoy.[77] Production at the two major installations was about 23,000 annually in the 1760's.[78] This was more than adequate when added to considerable stocks conserved in government arsenals. When the French occupied the international arms center of Liege in 1760, they contented themselves with banning the exportation of weapons from the city.[79] This seems a clear indication that domestic production was sufficient.

The infantry carried the model 1754 musket, a ponderous weapon weighing eleven pounds and firing a .69 caliber ball. It was similar to the arms of the other belligerents and was considered a thoroughly satisfactory weapon.[80] Its chief drawback was that it was largely handmade; consequently parts were not interchangeable. Repairs had to be made by professional armorers periodically dispatched to the armies for this purpose.[81] Though interchangeability of parts would have enhanced serviceability greatly, experiments made along this line were abandoned as impractical.[82]

In the hands of a well-trained soldier the musket could be fired three times a minute, which was the maximum rate

77. According to Manceau the British government sought to purchase 100,000 muskets from Charleville as late as 1791. *Charleville*, p. 32. Many countries were dependent upon foreign technical personnel for their own production as well; this was particularly true of Prussia and Russia. Gothsche, *Die königlichen Gewehrfabriken. Kurze Darstellung ihrer Entstehung, Entwicklung und Aufgaben* (Berlin, 1904), pp. 1–12; L. G. Beskrovnii, "Proizvodstvo Voruzheniia i Boepripasov na russkikh Zavodakh v pervoi Polovine XVIII v.," *Istoricheskie Zapiski*, No. 36 (1951), pp. 101–41.

78. Manceau, *Charleville*, p. 28; Gras, *Armurerie*, p. 39.

79. Joseph Fraikin, *L'industrie armurière liègeoise et le banc d'épreuves des armes à feu de Liège* (Liège, 1940), p. 36.

80. James E. Hicks and André Jandot, *Notes on French Ordnance, 1717– 1936* (Mount Vernon, N.Y., 1938), p. 9.

81. See in this connection Gayot's letter to Crémilles of July 30, 1758, Gayot MSS, 647–242.

82. The chief obstacle to true standardization was the lock, a mechanism scarcely six inches long but containing a score of intricate parts. Identical locks could indeed be made, but they required more than double the time it took to make ordinary ones. Moritz Meyer, *Manuel historique de la technologie des armes à feu*, trans. A. Rieffel (Paris, 1838), II, 84.

of fire in all armies.[83] Great stress was laid upon rapidity of fire. The hope of increasing firepower further led Paris Duverney to embark on a costly experiment with a breech-loading musket devised by an inventor named Bordier. The new weapon proved a failure and Bordier committed suicide, but not before several thousand of the useless muskets had been manufactured and sent to the armies.[84]

Accuracy with the musket was not great by modern standards and little emphasis was placed on it. If officers told their men to take aim, it was invariably at the middle of the enemy's body, regardless of the distance. In this connection an experience of Mercoyrol de Beaulieu is revealing. During the storming of a German town he imprudently donned the bonnet abandoned by a Hessian grenadier. Fifty French grenadiers mistook him for one of the enemy and fired on him at a distance of thirty paces. One ball clipped the bayonet from his musket and another passed harmlessly through his coat.[85]

In addition to the musket, the infantryman carried a saber and a bayonet, though these were seldom used. The bayonets, in particular, were regarded by the soldiers as useless impediments. The Prince de Ligne claimed that in all his years of warfare he had seen only one authentic bayonet encounter.[86] It is doubtful if the enemy made much better use of this weapon. Of the wounded soldiers admitted to the Invalides in 1762, only 9 per cent had been wounded by bayonets; over 80 per cent had been wounded by firearms.[87] Another largely useless weapon was the spontoon, or pike, which

---

83. The much vaunted rapidity of fire of the Prussian infantry was probably a myth. The figure of six loads per minute was achieved only in simulated drill. Werner Eckard and Otto Morawietz, *Die Handwaffen des brandenburgisch-preussisch-deutschen Heeres, 1640–1945* (Hamburg, 1957), p. 32.

84. A. Millot, "Le fusil à manivelle, 1758," *Carnet de la sabretache*, III (1895), 233–40.

85. *Campagnes*, p. 299.

86. Quoted in Delbrück, *Kriegskunst*, IV, 309, n. 1.

87. Corvisier, *Soldat*, p. 674.

infantry officers were supposed to carry. General Cornillon reported despairingly: "There is not a single spontoon remaining in the entire infantry." [88] The government bowed to the inevitable and ordered the officers to arm themselves with muskets.[89]

Regulations stipulated that cavalrymen carry a short musket, a pair of pistols, and a saber. In addition they were to wear as defensive armor a half-breastplate or *plastron*, and an iron skull cap inside their hats.[90] Cavalry officers were to wear complete breastplates, though as has been seen, the custom was more honored in the breach than in the observance.[91] The armament of the dragoons and hussars varied slightly from that of the cavalry. There were occasional complaints that the sabers were badly tempered and that they were not as long as those of the enemy. It is doubtful that many cavalrymen agreed with the observation of one officer that the valor of a nation could be measured in the shortness of its swords.[92]

The most serious deficiency in French armament lay in the artillery. To be sure, the armies were generously supplied with field pieces; unfortunately they were obsolete. Artillery was in process of rapid evolution in this period, becoming lighter and more maneuverable in keeping with the trend toward more mobile warfare. Progress in this direction was particularly marked in the eight years of peace from 1748 to 1756. At the beginning of the Seven Years' War the Austrian army was equipped with a new three pounder weighing only 430 pounds.[93] The Prussian three pounder,

88. Cornillon to Belle-Isle, April 7, 1758, A¹ 3510–69.
89. *Ordonnance du Roi concernant l'armement des officers et des sergeans des compagnies de fusiliers du 31 octobre 1758.*
90. Sautai and Desbrière, *Cavalerie*, pp. 13–15.
91. The practice may have been dictated as much by comfort as vanity. The physician Colombier said the *cuirasse* or breastplate was too heavy and troubled the respiration and constricted the shoulders and neck. *Code*, I, 131.
92. Sautai and Desbrière, *Cavalerie*, pp. 32–33; Dussauge, *Etudes*, p. 170.
93. Meyer, *Technologie*, I, 178.

developed in 1754, weighed 450 pounds.[94] By contrast, the comparable French four pounder weighed 1,000 pounds; its slightest displacement had to be made with horses. The same inordinate heaviness characterized the larger French pieces.[95]

The chief obstacle to correcting this unfortunate situation lay in the artillery officers themselves. The dean of the artillerists, M. de Vallière, was the chief defender of the old system. It had been established by his father in 1732, and no amount of argument could shake Vallière's filial respect. Critics were not lacking. They pointed out that the Vallière system ignored numerous innovations, such as standardized carriages with interchangeable parts, iron axles, limber boxes, and sights.[96] For two decades the debate raged between the "red" artillery officers who defended the system and the "blues" who wanted to abandon it. It was not until after Vallière's death in 1776 that the "blues" finally triumphed. The new system, that of Gribeauval, produced the admirable artillery which saved the Revolution at Valmy.

For the period of the Seven Years' War, the army was obliged to drag in its wake "a heavy and cumbersome matériel, paralytic pieces which stayed where they were once placed. Who lost the battle lost his cannon." [97] A few palliatives were tried. Each infantry battalion received a light four pounder, in imitation of the Prussian army, which had two light pieces per battalion.[98] Broglie, on his own initiative, had some of the Vallière pieces bored out to accept a larger ball.[99]

Munitions and other ordnance stores are seldom mentioned in the official correspondence. Generally these were kept in arsenals and shipped to the armies as the need arose. As a rule the army kept on hand a stock of two hundred rounds for each cannon and sixty rounds for each musket, in addition

94. Jany, *Geschichte*, II, 257.
95. Hicks and Jandot, *Notes*, p. 144.
96. Mention, *Saint Germain*, pp. 162–65.
97. *Ibid.*, p. 173.
98. Dussauge, *Etudes*, p. 167, n. 2.
99. *Ibid.*

to the sixty rounds that each soldier was to carry in his cartridge box.[100] The consumption of munitions was prodigious. In the first four months of 1758 the Army of the Lower Rhine received 400,000 pounds each of lead and powder.[101] Guibert estimated that in the average battle a half million musket rounds were fired.[102]

The most critical commodity in warfare of the era (excepting money) was potassium nitrate or saltpeter, the chief component of the gunpowder of that day. The government had asserted control over this chemical as early as the fifteenth century and had subsequently established a monopoly on the manufacture of powder. Characteristically, the industry was farmed to a private concern.[103] Saltpeter could be found in natural deposits and on the walls and in the cellars of dwellings. The concessionaires had the right of search in homes and premises, a practice so irksome to the population that it was later suppressed by Turgot. Saltpeter was never plentiful, particularly if one relied on natural deposits supplemented by importation. By mid-eighteenth century artificial methods of production were developed; several countries, Prussia and Sweden particularly, began to construct *nitrières*—walled enclosures or pits something on the order of compost piles— as early as 1748. Artificial production of this critical commodity in France seems not to have been used to any extent until some thirty years later.[104]

100. Guibert, *Tactique*, I, 501.
101. Belle-Isle to Clermont, April 27, 1758, A¹ 3501–299.
102. *Tactique*, I, 501.
103. For an excellent account of the development of the gunpowder monopoly see "Le service des poudres," *Revue historique de l'armée,* XIX, No. 2 (1964), 85–108.
104. See in this connection the long and valuable article, "Salpêtrier," in Panckoucke's *Encyclopédie méthodique: Arts et métiers mécaniques* (Paris, 1786), 166–212.

10

Transport and Communications

From the preceding chapter it should be clear that no eighteenth-century army could hope to live off the areas in which it operated save as a last desperate expedient. Armies had grown too large, and their needs too complex. Each army was "bound with chains to its magazines."[1] Consequently the supply columns which linked the depot and the army in the field were an indispensable element in military operations. The transport system was a transitional one; while the military no longer supplied their needs by haphazard seizure of civilian transport, they still had no adequate transport of their own. Movement of supplies depended upon co-operation among military and civil functionaries, civilian contractors, and reluctant peasants.[2]

In the French army the movement of troops and their equipment within the realm was accomplished by means of the *étape*. The inhabitants along certain routes were required to feed and shelter soldiers and to supply wagons and teams to haul military goods. Though this onerous task was often commuted to a money tax and performed by an entrepreneur, it figures among the grievances in the *cahiers* in 1789.[3] In Germany French transport was secured by several means.

1. Baumann, *Verpflegung*, I, 281.
2. A. Pernot, *Aperçu historique sur le service des transports militaires* (Paris and Limoges, 1894), is authoritative but brief on the eighteenth century; see pp. 66–77.
3. See "Arrêt du 25 decembre 1759," Archives Nat. E 2680–187; Audouin, *Administration*, III, 214.

The army owned few vehicles; though the artillery had some, the horses and civilian drivers were supplied by contract. Most of the companies which supplied the army provided transport for their commodities as well, but the government assumed the task of shipping stores for the hospitals and purchased or rented the horses and wagons used by the *munitionnaires*.[4] Whenever possible these were obtained by requisition.

The generals and intendants brought what order they could to the movements of this conglomeration of vehicles. They stipulated supply routes, established the order of march for convoys, and provided armed escorts and detachments of the *prévôté* to police them. Each regiment had its *vaguemestre,* usually its major, and each of the logistical services had wagonmasters as well. The government required that all vehicles used for army service be four-wheeled and drawn by four horses.[5]

Transport of goods by private enterprise never worked well. During the winter of 1758–1759, the government negotiated with a single concern for the delivery of all goods ordered by the regiments for their *réparations*. This exclusive contract proved a poor arrangement, for the contractors still had not made delivery in April, 1759.[6] The company which undertook to supply horses and drivers for the artillery either could not or would not meet the demands placed upon it. Cannon were sometimes lost because the unreliable civilian drivers would refuse to move them in the middle of a battle. At Clostercamp they fled the field with their teams; artillery officers had to chase them and bring them back by force.[7] The heavy Vallière pieces were partly at fault. Their displacement required large teams and rapidly exhausted what

4. Paulmy to Gayot, Feb. 25, 1758, Gayot MSS, 640–235; Guibert, *Tactique,* II, 278, n. 1.

5. Pernot, *Aperçu,* pp. 62–63.

6. Broglie to Belle-Isle, April 7, 1759, A¹ 3914–63.

7. Le Pelletier, *Mémoires,* p. 125.

horses the entrepreneurs could find. Guibert estimated that transporting 400 field pieces and their appurtenances would require 2,400 vehicles and 9,600 horses.[8]

The problem of transport was rendered considerably more difficult by the exorbitant demands which troops and officers made upon the facilities. Each battalion was permitted two wagons to haul tents and cooking gear, but in practice the soldiers commandeered many more for this purpose.[9] The officers had an even worse record. Between 1690 and 1757 there were no fewer than seven *ordonnances* limiting the number of horses and vehicles officers could take into the field. The very frequency of legislation indicates how little attention was paid to it. The regulations seem liberal enough: a lieutenant general could keep thirty horses and three conveyances; a *maréchal-de-camp* could have twenty horses and two vehicles.[10] Yet it was not uncommon for a general officer to maintain a stable of fifty mounts; the Count of Gisors had twenty-three, though as a colonel he was entitled to only sixteen. Even so, he complained that he was the only colonel in the army without at least one carriage.[11] Much transport was used to supply the luxuries for which the French camp was well known. When the Prussians seized the headquarters of Soubise at Gotha, they found in the officers' baggage pet monkeys and parrots, mountains of silverware, and whole cases of lavender water, wrist bands, and other such trifles.[12] Officers had a bad habit of appropriating the nearest vehicles in sight for their own purposes, even those used to carry the

8. *Tactique,* I, 466. Broglie pleaded desperately but in vain for two hundred additional field pieces for the campaign of 1760; the entrepreneurs could not find the horses necessary to transport them from the arsenals. Mention, *Saint Germain,* Introduction, p. xxi.

9. "De toutes les voitures qu'on a demandé dans le pays, il n'en a pas été fourni le quart, et ce quart a été enlevé dans les chemins par les régiments." General Monteynard to Broglie, March 24, 1758, A¹ 3473–172.

10. *Ordonnance du 9 mai 1757.*

11. Rousset, *Gisors,* pp. 182–83.

12. Pernot, *Aperçu,* p. 68.

mails.[13] When Clermont left Versailles for the army in the spring of 1758, he encountered a steady stream of officers returning to France in commandeered conveyances.[14] When Hameln was abandoned the artillery officers used the wagons to evacuate their baggage, leaving their pontoons to the enemy.[15]

Along with each army there also moved a large number of wagons belonging to sutlers, *vivandières,* and other camp followers. The modest force which Soubise took to Rosbach had no fewer than 12,000 of these in its train.[16] Curiously the hordes of these enterprising civilians were seldom the objects of complaint. Perhaps the generals regarded them as a secondary supply system. The *prévôté* assigned numbers to their wagons and tried to keep them in order. When they got in the way, they were given short shrift. The *prévôté* simply cut their traces and left them to their own devices.[17]

Requisition of vehicles in Germany was constantly used, but the yield was always disappointingly low.[18] The Imperial Capitulation of 1734 permitted the auxiliaries of Austria to obtain transport from members of the Empire at a fixed rental rate.[19] But the French had little money and took no care of the few vehicles they could obtain by this means. French generals were instructed to use force if necessary to obtain transport, after going through the formality of letters of requisition; for, as the minister told them: "Above all, the service must not fail." [20]

Despite the most rigorous measures the transport system

13. Clermont to Belle-Isle, Feb. 7, 1758, A¹ 3500–210.
14. Clermont to Pompadour, Feb. 7, 1758, A² 35–39.
15. Belle-Isle to Clermont, April 6, 1758, A² 36–152.
16. Pernot, *Aperçu,* p. 65, n. 1.
17. Cornillon to Belle-Isle, June 11, 1759, A¹ 3517–147.
18. "J'écris des politesses, d'autres fois je menace, et rien ne réussit." Contades to Belle-Isle, Oct. 17, 1758, A¹ 3485–18.
19. The stipulations of this accord are found in Bernis' letter to Paulmy of Jan. 6, 1758, A² 56–83.
20. Belle-Isle to Contades, June 9, 1759, A¹ 3917–106.

remained inadequate. In the official correspondence its failings are manifest at every turn. Nearly half a million rations of forage lay rotting at Wesel because there were no wagons to move them to the Rhine, only five leagues away.[21] When the French abandoned Hanover early in 1758, several thousand sick and wounded had to be left behind.[22] Even those who were evacuated were later removed from their conveyances because these were needed to haul bread.[23] There was hardly enough transport for everyday needs; so when an emergency arose, for example when a depot had to be abandoned, goods either had to be destroyed or left to the enemy. For this reason vast stores were lost at Dusseldorf and at Lippstadt.[24]

The horse was indispensable to eighteenth-century warfare, though its full importance has yet to be studied.[25] The demand was one that was never satisfied in wartime. Nor was the problem exclusively a French one. Frederick, who sought horses from as far away as Poland and the Ukraine, never seemed to have enough of them. The price for a good horse doubled in Prussia during the war; by the spring of 1761 the Prussian artillery alone was short 3,400.[26] The Russian government, which had often sought to obtain its military provisions through a tax in kind, even attempted to meet its needs in horses this way. This curious "horse tax" was so unproductive and hard on the peasantry that it was abandoned at the beginning of the war.[27]

Mortality rates for horses were very high. The *munition-*

21. Paulmy to M. Vaugine, Jan. 9, 1758, Gayot MSS, 639–241.
22. Gayot to Paulmy, Feb. 27, 1758, Gayot MSS, 641–15.
23. Broglie to Clermont, March 26, 1758, A¹ 3473–185.
24. "Etat général de tous les effets qui existaient à Dusseldorff et qui ont été abandonnés le 8 juillet 1758 lors de l'évacuation de la place par les troupes françaises et palatines, dans les magazins des effets du Roy, dans ceux des vivres, des fourages, du bois de chauffage, et de l'hôpital ambulant," Gayot MSS, 648–131; Guibert, *Tactique*, II, 298.
25. For the Prussian service there is E. O. Mentzel, *Die Remontirung der preussischen Armee in ihrer historischer Entwicklung* (Berlin, 1870).
26. Jany, *Geschichte*, II, 602.
27. Beskrovnii, *Russkaia Armiia*, pp. 125–27.

naires used a total of 22,776 during the conflict, but had only 3,500 on hand at its conclusion.[28] In the summer of 1758 the cavalry regiments of the Army of the Lower Rhine had 8,235 serviceable mounts and 2,202 unfit; 2,545 were lacking altogether.[29] Although the government allowed two hundred and fifty livres for each remount, the captains found that a suitable horse cost twice that. The minister often had to come to the aid of the most destitute units with extra money or horses from the royal stables and *haras*.[30] In most cases, however, the burden fell upon the captains.[31] When a struggling young officer like Castelnau lost his own mount, he faced a financial catastrophe. Replacing it would put him in debt for three years.[32]

The quality of French horseflesh was only mediocre at best, according to Guibert.[33] In any event the quantity was not sufficient for war needs. Many units bought abroad; the artillery in Germany and Switzerland, the *munitionnaires* in Brabant.[34] There were frequent complaints over the poor quality of horses. Though regulations required that cavalry mounts be at least four feet, nine inches at the withers, this was often not observed. Artillery horses were so small and weak that one officer referred to them as "sheep." [35] There was little chance for discriminate buying; this was particularly unfortunate for the cavalry, where horses were supposed to be

---

28. "Mémoires historiques," 230–32.
29. "Etat de la Situation de la Cavalerie de l'Armée du Rhin au 13 aout 1758," A¹ 3520–209.
30. Contades to Belle-Isle, Dec. 19, 1758, A¹ 3489–17.
31. The fact that the cavalry captain owned the horses in his company had serious effects upon tactics. While the Prussian cavalry charged at a gallop, the French cavalry still charged at a trot—a much less effective maneuver, but one which spared horseflesh. See in this connection Sautai and Desbrière, *Cavalerie,* p. 9; Delbrück, *Kriegskunst,* IV, 325–26.
32. Letter to Gaix, June 16, 1758, *Lettres,* p. 61.
33. *Tactique,* I, 393. For a comparison of horseflesh in various countries, see De Boussanelle, *Observations militaires* (Paris, 1761), pp. 132–226.
34. Guibert, *Tactique,* I, 466; "Observation sur la position des vivres à l'époque du 23 mai 1760," A¹ 3554–200.
35. Hoegger, *Neujahrsblatt der Feuerwerken Gesellschaft in Zürich,* CXXXXVII, 23.

of different ages, so that replacement would be gradual.[36] The arduous nature of the service and the scarcity of forage probably accounted for more losses than combat. Unquestionably cavalry mounts bore too heavy a load—350 pounds.[37] Fortunately the army was spared the supreme disaster, an epidemic of glanders. Whenever this malady appeared the unit involved was immediately isolated and the infected animals killed. Sometimes an entire regiment was withdrawn from the line to prevent contagion.[38]

In logistics one problem tends to create others. The chronic shortage of forage forced the government to immobilize much of its transport during the inactive months. In the winter the armies kept only the absolute minimum of horses, sending thousands back to winter in France.[39] This meant that the forces were almost paralyzed in the event of winter fighting; moreover the next spring's campaign could not begin until the horses were brought back. In 1759 and 1760 the opening of the campaign was delayed appreciably for this reason.[40]

One cannot leave the subject of transport without qualifying somewhat the appalling picture that has emerged so far. It is true that the system, which had been perfected in Louis XIV's Dutch wars, was outmoded. It is also true that the *ordonnances* of the 1670's and 1680's which had created it were still in force in 1756 and indeed in 1789. Yet all the other belligerents used the same or similar expedients and found themselves likewise hampered in their operations by logistical fetters. If the French were particularly embarrassed in this regard, it was at least partly due to other considerations. The mania for *luxe* in the camp and field, which can hardly be exaggerated, kept the roads filled with thousands of wagons hauling trifles when they might have been hauling essentials.

36. Ray, *Réflexions*, p. 202.

37. Sautai and Desbrière, *Cavalerie*, p. 36. See also Guibert, *Tactique*, I, 370–71.

38. Contades to Belle-Isle, June 20, 1759, A¹ 3517–258.

39. In the winter of 1759–1760 Broglie kept only one hundred horses per squadron. Bourcet, *Mémoires*, I, 243.

40. See Contades to Belle-Isle, May 5, 1759, A¹ 3515–45; Broglie to Belle-Isle, May 22, 1760, A¹ 3554–191.

From the logistical point of view, the French armies were probably too large. Much of the campaigning was done in areas of Germany where roads were poor, waterways few, populations hostile, and local transport facilities virtually nonexistent. The smaller armies of Frederick and Ferdinand could profit from interior lines. Local populations were generally friendly and supplied teams and wagons without which they would have been hamstrung.[41]

The communications system, like most other services, was largely in the hands of entrepreneurs. In this case the service was confided to a company organized by the wealthy Thiroux family, serving as sub-farmers of the *Postes et Messageries de France*. Their contract provided that they would convey all official communications between the field armies and the court, and also handle the private correspondence to and from the field. The contractors agreed to carry all official correspondence free of charge by regular service. Special couriers could be dispatched using their facilities, but in this case the expenses were paid by the government. In addition the company paid the government 5,001,500 livres annually for its concession. The revenues from private correspondence carried to the armies went to the government, and the company collected the postage on letters moving in the other direction.[42] This latter revenue was the chief source of income. for the company.[43]

There is little reference to the work of these entrepreneurs in the official correspondence; the inference is that generally the service was considered satisfactory. The time required for transmission of letters to and from the field varied from three to seven days, depending upon the army's position and the weather conditions. The court was content to wait a

41. The Prussians still relied heavily upon help from the local population. See Jany, *Geschichte*, II, 272.
42. A copy of this contract, dated April 1, 1757, is to be found in Belle-Isle's letter to Gayot of Sept. 23, 1758, Gayot MSS, 648–233.
43. The postage on a private letter was twenty sous. Castelnau, *Lettres*, p. 156, n. 1. This rather high rate may help to explain the dearth of letters from soldiers and the lower grades of officers.

reasonable time for news, but grew highly indignant if it was not the first to learn of developments in Germany. When the minister learned of the fall of Bremen from a Dutch journal, or was officially apprised of the abandonment of Minden twenty-four hours after it was known in Paris, his wrath usually fell upon the shoulders of a luckless general.[44] The field commanders were constantly urged to write at least every other day in order that the ministry could give lie to the gossip and rumors which were always circulating.[45]

The main difficulties were encountered in lateral communications—those which passed along the army's front in the campaign months and between garrisons during winter quarters. The postal employees were sometimes not informed of troop movements by the *maréchal général*.[46] Communications between armies or detachments often failed because the intervening territory was dominated by the enemy, who intercepted the couriers. In February, 1758, Clermont received only three of the ten couriers dispatched from Saint Germain's garrison.[47] Saint Germain had received no instructions for a week, and was convinced that the peasants were waylaying the couriers.[48] To maintain the security of their correspondence the field commanders were supplied with a *chiffre* or code. The cumbersome and time-consuming system was seldom used.[49] Ironically it was the incompetent Soubise who was most diligent in encoding his dispatches.

---

44. See Belle-Isle's letters to Clermont, March 7 and 23, 1758, A¹ 3473–49, 170. Broglie was severely reprimanded when it was discovered that he had instructed his couriers to deliver letters to his family before taking official dispatches to the ministry. See Belle-Isle to Broglie, Aug. 8, 1760, A¹ 3558–98.
    45. Belle-Isle to Clermont, March 12, 1758, A¹ 3473–89.
    46. "Mémoire pour les Postes de l'Armée, 8 avril 1758," A¹ 3501–216.
    47. Clermont to Saint Germain, March 4, 1758, A² 35–108.
    48. Saint Germain to Clermont, March 2, 1758, A² 39–107.
    49. A copy of the code used in 1760 is found in Serie A⁴, Carton LXXXVII, No. 100. It comprises nine hundred numbers with word, syllable, or number equivalents. The encoding portion is arranged as follows: ab—31, able—122, abandon—143, etc. The decoding portion is similarly ordered: 1—Hildesheim, 2—assurer, ance, 3—l'Elbe, 4—au, aux, etc.

In sum the military communications system operated fairly satisfactorily by eighteenth-century standards. It was far superior to the transport system, whose deficiencies plagued the armies at every turn.

11

The Medical Services

By the time of the Seven Years' War the medical services of the French Army had been in existence some two hundred years.[1] In the period under study there were three distinct services: regimental medical facilities were headed by a surgeon-major, with each company having a "frater" or barber-surgeon and an *aumônier* or chaplain, whose duties might be medical as well as spiritual;[2] *hôpitaux sédentaires* were placed in various French and German towns; finally, there were the *hôpitaux ambulants,* mobile units which followed the armies in the field.

The hospitals provided the great bulk of care for the seriously ill; characteristically both types were operated *à l'entreprise.* In the Army of the Lower Rhine the *hôpital ambulant* was in the hands of a *régie,* while the *hôpitaux sédentaires* were confided to a private company. A contract for this latter service has survived and serves to illustrate how the system was organized.

The entrepreneurs were to feed the patient in carefully specified portions; the bread was to be of pure wheat "of good quality and well baked," and the meat was to contain no "heads, hearts, tripes, or feet." Each patient was to be given a ration of white wine, unless the physicians prescribed

1. Brief resumés of the evolution of this service can be found in Docteur Léon-Raoul-Marie Brice and Capitaine Maurice Bottet, *Le corps de santé militaire en France, son evolution—ses campagnes, 1708–1882* (Paris and Nancy, 1907), pp. 1–50; and Jean des Cilleuls, "L'organisation du service de santé aux armées de l'ancien régime," *Revue historique de l'armée,* IX, No. 2 (1953), 7–36.

2. Mention, *Saint Germain,* p. 233; Jean des Cilleuls, "Les aumôniers aux armées de l'ancien régime," *Revue historique de l'armée,* XII, No. 3 (1956), pp. 5–16.

red wine instead. The contract goes on to specify in great detail the various furnishings, including the bedding, which was to be changed every fifteen days. For his ministrations the entrepreneur received a daily emolument of twenty-five sous for each soldier in his charge, and fifty for each officer. For each burial he was entitled to forty sous. The government's interests were well protected. The entrepreneur could be fined for any shortcoming, and his administration was done under the watchful eyes of a *commissaire des guerres* and of the medical staff, which was paid by the king.[3]

The company which maintained the *hôpitaux sédentaires* at the beginning of the war possessed all the vices of the contract system at its worst. The directors of the company were "partly men of probity without intelligence and partly men of intelligence without probity."[4] The representatives in the field were likewise unsuited to their task. The director of the hospitals was M. de Montlys, too old and too incapable to perform his functions adequately. His assistants, MM. Savary and Stoffel, "appear to know very little of their functions, and hardly concern themselves with anything save the interests of the company."[5] The service fell into chaos. "The hospitals were slaughterhouses," wrote Guibert. "I will say no more; I do not wish to soil my pen in cataloguing these crimes."[6] Nor was Guibert the only witness to the appalling conditions of the hospitals. An inspection of the installations at Cologne revealed that the sick were packed three to a bed.[7]

The constant stream of alarming reports from the field led the minister to take drastic action. He voided the contract with the company and negotiated a new agreement with another concern. The new entrepreneurs promised well: "I

3. "Marché pour les hopitaux de l'Armée du Bas Rhin, 30 avril 1758," Gayot MSS, 643–66.
4. Paris Duverney to Gayot, May 18, 1758, Gayot MSS, 642–110.
5. Gayot to Paulmy, March 15, 1758, Gayot MSS, 640–256.
6. *Tactique*, II, 267.
7. "Mémoire sur l'Hopital établi dans le convent des Augustins de la ville de Cologne" (no date), Gayot MSS, 642–357. See also Rousset, *Gisors*, pp. 374–75.

have . . . tried to form a company which could better perform this service; most of those who compose it are rich and have some reputation, the others are intelligent and seem well qualified." [8] The complaints about the *hôpitaux sédentaires* continued, but with less frequency. The new company seems to have done its best to provide service.

The hospital system was beset by numerous obstacles not of its own making. Many of the German princes refused to permit the establishments in their towns, and forced the French to use small villages with totally inadequate facilities.[9] The mobile hospital *régie* suffered especially from the critical shortage of transport. Both hospital systems had difficulty obtaining adequate supplies; the meat which was delivered to them was sometimes spoiled.[10] The facilities were frequently not sufficient to treat the large numbers of sick and wounded. In February, 1758, the Army of the Lower Rhine had 14,102 hospitalized in the infantry alone.[11] To relieve the pressure on the overcrowded hospitals the government permitted the regiments to establish their own installations, granting a few hundred livres to each regiment for this purpose.[12] Occasionally the army placed its sick and wounded in German hospitals, paying about twenty sous a day for each patient they accepted.[13] When the army could not evacuate its hospitals before an enemy advance, the entrepreneurs were obliged to maintain installations behind enemy lines, a practice which entailed much difficulty and extra expenditure.

Of all the problems which the hospital directors faced, the most serious was the lack of funds. Before being paid for their services the company and *régie* had to go through a

8. Belle-Isle to Gayot, May 7, 1758, Gayot MSS, 643–4.
9. See Gayot's "Observations sur les hopitaux de l'Armée du Bas Rhin" (no date), Gayot MSS, 650–54.
10. Broglie to Belle-Isle, May 15, 1760, A¹ 3554–109.
11. Out of a total force of 76,341 infantrymen. "Etat de la composition des régiments d'infanterie de l'Armée du Bas Rhin commandé par M. le Cte de Clermont au premier février 1758," A² 35–63. The figures for the cavalry for the same period have not survived.
12. Crémilles to Gayot, March 23, 1758, Gayot MSS, 641–190.
13. Gayot to M. Gillot de Vireux, April 4, 1758, Gayot MSS, 641–202.

cumbersome accounting system required by the government. The hospital directors had to compute the total sum due them by reckoning the patient-days over a period of a month. This was then examined by a *commissaire des guerres* and submitted for payment. In practice the harried hospital officials did not have sufficient time to make these calculations and fell behind in their accounts. In June, 1758, they had been unable to submit a statement since the end of the campaign of 1757.[14] By 1759 the records were so hopelessly confused that the government agreed to pay an arbitrary figure for hospitalized soldiers, reckoning them at one-twentieth of the effectives.[15]

The government could simplify the accounting system but it could not draw money from an empty treasury. Nowhere did the poverty of the government have more disastrous results than in the operation of the hospitals. In 1760 the company which maintained the *hôpitaux sédentaires* had received no payment from the government in many months. It had borrowed to the limit of its credit and could get no more funds from any source. It was forced into bankruptcy with an indebtedness of 6,200,000 livres. The government stood by a helpless witness to the calamity.[16]

The picture is black indeed. Yet the French army possessed the best and most extensive medical facilities in Europe. Paris Duverney boasted with pardonable pride: "The French nation is perhaps the only one which has the practice of maintaining hospitals with the armies; other nations, repelled by the attendant difficulties, do without these, at the expense of human life." [17] This conclusion was echoed by contemporaries and has been confirmed by modern historians.[18] England

14. Crémilles to Gayot, June 1, 1758, Gayot MSS, 645–34.
15. *Arrest du Conseil d'Etat du Roi, portant Règlement pour les déductions des journées d'Hopitaux, à faire sur les troupes de Sa Majesté, pendant l'année 1757 les six premiers mois de 1758, du 2 fevrier 1759,* in the collection *Ordonnances militaires* previously cited.
16. Belle-Isle to Broglie, May 20, 1760, A¹ 3554–166.
17. Paris Duverney to Clermont, May 16, 1758, Gayot MSS, 634–104.
18. Colombier held that the French hospitals were the model for the

produced probably the greatest single figure in eighteenth-century military medicine—Sir John Pringle; [19] yet the British army's facilities were still "largely extemporaneous" at the time of the American Revolution.[20] It was not until the end of the century that Sir John Hunter put the British army on a par with other armies in this regard.[21] Prussia, too, seems to have been relatively backward. Most of the medical regulations dated from the reign of Frederick William I.[22] Apparently the service depended largely on the *Feldscheerer* or barber-surgeon; Frederick II mobilized only four physicians in 1756.[23] Though he introduced an *hôpital ambulant,* the Prussian medical service had little or no transport of its own. The wounded were hauled from the battlefield in bread wagons or whatever other conveyances could be found.[24] Perhaps Frederick had a low opinion of the medical profession in general; [25] in any event he did not order a drastic overhaul of the medical service until the last year of his life.[26] The mortal-

rest of Europe. *Code,* III, iii. Both Frederick William and Frederick II had sought French medical personnel for service with their army. Emil Knorr, *Entwicklung und Gestaltung des Heeres-Sanitätswesens der Europäischen Staaten* (Hanover, 1880), pp. 74, 80. See also Delbrück, *Kriegskunst,* IV, 270.

19. Pringle, whom Colombier called "the Prince of Military Medicine," was the author of *Observations on the Diseases of the Army* (London, 1751). This work, published and translated many times, became the *vade mecum* of the practitioners of military medicine.

20. Curtis, *British Army,* pp. 11–12.

21. Knorr, *Sanitätswesen,* p. 342.

22. Including one which forbade the removal of wounded from the battlefield until the fighting was over. *Ibid.,* p. 82.

23. Jany, *Geschichte,* II, 215.

24. Knorr, *Sanitätswesen,* p. 84.

25. He once claimed to have cured his army of dysentery after his physicians had given up; his remedy was a tartar emetic dissolved in water. *Ibid.,* pp. 85–86.

26. See in this connection Lieutenant Colonel Robert S. Moses, "Of Plagues and Pennants," *Military Review,* XLV, No. 5 (May, 1965), 71–84. Moses contends that Frederick saw the need for better medical facilities only after the "Potato War" of 1778–1779. Though there was no fighting to speak of, the Prussians lost 15,000 men, mostly to disease. Knorr by contrast emphasizes Frederick's concern and "humanity," but his defense of the Prussian monarch is too strenuous to be very convincing. *Sanitätswesen,* pp. 82–91 *passim.*

ity rate in the Prussian army was high: the Jung-Braun-schweig Regiment, with a normal complement of about 1,800 men, lost a total of 4,474 from 1756 to 1763. Only 700 of these were deserters; the rest were victims of wounds or disease.[27] This may be something of a record, and certainly an unenviable one.

Whether motivated by humanitarian considerations or a less noble self-interest, the ministry always displayed a deep concern over the health of the troops. The physicians and surgeons which it recruited to supervise the medical services were generally of very high caliber.[28] It was the solicitude of the government which prompted it to raise the bread ration by four ounces and to supply meat during the entire year. It strongly urged the therapeutic practice of putting vinegar in the soldiers' drinking water.[29] It tested Dr. André's medicinal catheters at the Invalides and then sent 1,500 to the army with instructions for their use.[30] Alarmed at the high incidence of venereal disease, it prescribed Dr. Kayser's pills, and offered to dispatch Kayser himself to the front to supervise their use.[31] When the armies entered winter quarters special instructions were issued. The *chambrées* or quartering units were not to be too closely crowded in their rooms. The rooms were to be aired twice a day, and the temperature kept down. The soldiers were to purify their water by boiling it with a piece of rusty iron. The troops were to be exercised every day, but were warned to keep their coats buttoned and cover their mouths on going outside, "it being certain that the cold air received through the mouth directly attacks the chest." [32] Mercifully there were no major outbreaks of typhus or cholera such as had occurred in previous wars. Even so, the number

27. Jany, *Geschichte*, II, 666–67.
28. Doctors Andouillé, Colombier, and Richard, among others, figure prominently in Michaud's *Biographie universelle.*
29. Belle-Isle to Contades, July 5, 1759, A[1] 3518–64.
30. Crémilles to Gayot, Oct. 10, 1758, Gayot MSS, 649–148.
31. Belle-Isle to Gayot, April 19, 1758, Gayot MSS, 642–99.
32. "Mémoire pour servir d'instruction sur les moyens de conserver la santé des troupes pendant les quartiers d'hiver, 18 octobre 1757," A[2] 33–78.

of soldiers carried as sick and wounded was always sizable.[33] Invariably, the *états* for the cavalry show a lower rate of men incapacitated, confirming the popular view that this branch of the service was "healthier." [34]

The chief cause for the high mortality was neither bloody battles, nor unscrupulous entrepreneurs, nor the lack of money, but rather the appalling state of eighteenth-century medicine. Battle wounds claimed relatively few lives. While the limited nature of eighteenth-century warfare has perhaps been exaggerated, the battles in which the French fought do indicate a degree of *mollesse*. Casualty rates for major battles, of which there were perhaps two per year, are seldom more than 10 per cent. The figures were based upon the number who did not show up for roll call after the battle, and undoubtedly contain a large number of men who accidentally or intentionally got separated from their units. As one might suspect, disease was the great killer. Corvisier cites the case of a hospital in Aix-la-Chapelle which recorded 229 deaths from December, 1758, to December, 1762. Of these only seven were attributed to battle wounds. Two hundred and seven were caused by "fever." [35] It was often observed that the number of deaths was higher in the winter months when the armies were not fighting.[36]

Even the best appointed hospitals were charnel houses. Colombier estimated that for every hundred soldiers hospitalized, sixty were lost for the rest of the campaign, and forty of those were lost forever.[37] Soldiers instinctively feared the hospitals and preferred to stay with their regiments whenever

---

33. Colombier estimated that an army of 100,000 would always have a minimum of 1,200 in the *hôpital ambulant;* their transport would require 1,200 horses and 400 wagons. *Code,* II, 275. The Prussian regulations of September 16, 1787, instructed medical personnel to count on 10 per cent of the effectives as the minimum of sick and wounded; battles and epidemics would double or treble the number. Knorr, *Sanitätswesen,* p. 91.

34. Corvisier, *Soldat,* p. 161.

35. *Ibid.,* p. 686.

36. *Ibid.*

37. *Code,* II, 299.

they could, a fact that must be taken into consideration when examining the *états*.[38] Contagion was common, since usually the only patients isolated were those with venereal disease. Officers who felt compelled to visit the wards were advised to take a drink of brandy before entering and to keep a handkerchief before their faces while inside. The practice may have afforded some protection to the visitor, but could hardly have been reassuring to the patients.[39]

The *hôpital ambulant* was particularly hard on its patients, since it was often housed in barns and other ill-suited buildings and was obliged to transport its charges frequently in whatever vehicles could be found. In such conditions, one wonders whether this ambitious but inept medical service did not compound the evils it was supposed to cure. It is significant that Colombier touches upon battle wounds not at all, but devotes three volumes to baffling afflictions like "dropsy of the chest" and "hepatic fluxes," which were felling soldiers by the thousands.

38. *Ibid.,* 294; Corvisier, *Soldat,* p. 659.
39. Colombier, *Code,* I, 222.

Conclusion

What can be said in sum of the military establishment of the old regime? It is all too easy to condemn its shortcomings from a distance of two centuries—centuries which have seen tremendous progress in warfare, that most taxing of all human efforts. Conversely, the historian always runs the risk of becoming too enamored of his subject, and by a process of *rétroactivité sentimentale,* endowing it with qualities which it never possessed.

The French military establishment in the middle of the eighteenth century partook of the imperfections of all human institutions. Certain of its features were very advanced for their day, and justly excited the admiration of Europe. In many respects the French war machine very closely resembled those of the other great powers. The conclusion is inescapable, however, that in several very critical areas the French waged war with methods that were dangerously outmoded. In no small way this accounts for the failure of French arms during the Seven Years' War.

To a large degree the army suffered from the weaknesses of the monarchy itself. The destitute government was financially unable to bear its burdens adequately, and could not lavish on its armies the money that has rightly been called the sinews of war. The confusion, cabal, and irresponsibility that held sway in the field were merely transplanted from Versailles. The class antagonisms so detrimental to the army were those of the nation in general. What was everywhere lacking was the strong hand that could erase privilege, that could reduce chaos to order and disparity to uniformity. This strong hand could only have been that of an all-powerful

minister or a philosopher king. Neither of these was destined
to appear in the declining years of the monarchy.

At the beginning of the war the military establishment was
in a sense the captive of its own past achievements. The
machine that had yielded such glorious results for Condé,
Turenne, and Villars was fondly expected to provide the
recipe for victory once more. As the war continued there
arose a spirit of criticism and dissatisfaction—a development
which was perhaps but one aspect of the trend of thought in
the nation generally. The years following the war were a period of great agitation and ferment in military circles. A spate
of books appeared—nearly a hundred in the decade after
1760—whose authors subjected nearly every aspect of the
military establishment to close scrutiny. Numerous *Pensées,
Observations,* and *Réflexions* pointed out faults and suggested
changes in staff service, militia, tactics, artillery, fortifications,
mountain and partisan warfare, and a host of other matters.

The necessity for renovation was felt on the ministerial
level and often translated into action. Indeed Belle-Isle's various measures constitute an embryonic reform program during the war itself. In the last thirty years of the old regime's
existence there were three major periods of activity, corre-
sponding to the ministries of Choiseul (1761–1770), Saint
Germain (1775–1777), and Puységur (1788–1789).[1]

At first view the list of changes is impressive. The most
striking reform was the abolition of proprietary rights of of-

1. The attempts to reform the army can only be touched here in the
briefest detail. The best general account of military policy in the last
years of the old regime can be found in Captain Albert Latreille, *L'armée
et la nation à la fin de l'ancien régime. Les derniers ministres de la
guerre de la monarchie* (Paris, 1914). For Choiseul's reforms, see Vicomte
de Montbas, "Choiseul et la résurrection de l'armée de Rossbach," *Revue
des transactions de l'académie des sciences morales et politiques,* année 107
(1954), pp. 48–62. Saint Germain's ministry is covered in Mention, *Saint
Germain.* An excellent account of the innovations of the Conseil de la
Guerre in 1787–1789 is to be found in Jean Egret, *La Pré-Révolution française (1787–1788)* (Paris, 1962), pp. 73–94. For the movement of ideas in
military circles see Eugène Carrias, *La pensée militaire française* (Paris,
1960), pp. 156–89.

ficers over their units. Since the government was unable to purchase the units outright, it was decided that the price should be reduced by one-quarter each time ownership changed. The process was thus a gradual one, still not completed by 1789.

The soldier's pay was increased, his uniform standardized, and his housing improved by the construction of barracks. The government intervened in company and regimental administration to secure adequate training and discipline. The number of regiments was fixed permanently, with separate peacetime and wartime footings. A great amount of attention was given to the training of officers. General Bourcet opened the first staff school in the 1760's. The Ecole Militaire and the cavalry school at Saumur saw to the training of line officers. A series of measures in the 1780's further perfected the medical facilities.

Armament was greatly improved by the introduction of the Gribeauval system, championed by Choiseul. The infantry received the model 1777 musket; the arsenals were emptied of obsolete small arms (many of which went to the American revolutionaries). The new weapons system saw service in all the wars of the Revolution and Empire. The musket was not changed again until 1816; the artillery was not replaced until 1825.

Unfortunately the reform of the army did not proceed without interruption and retrogression. After the disgrace of Choiseul the portfolio of war passed to Monteynard, who undid much of his predecessor's work. Saint Germain was followed by Montbarrey, who in the words of a contemporary, "treated the military much too lightly, and was more given to his pleasures and intrigues than to his duty." [2]

The result of these frequent changes in ministers and policies (there were twelve ministers of war from 1760 to 1790)

2. Charles de Mathei, marquis de Valfons, *Souvenirs du marquis de Valfons, vicomte de Sébourg, lieutenant général des armées du Roi (1710–1786)* (Paris, 1906), p. 402.

was that much of the ground gained was subsequently lost; impermanence became a permanent feature of the military establishment. Choiseul sought to free the army's logistical service from the *régie* and the entrepreneur, but his successor restored them both and went so far as to abolish the post of military intendant. Saint Germain took up the battle in his turn, but his gains too were only temporary. It was not until 1788 that the army was once again authorized to provide its own food, forage, and uniforms.

The militia underwent constant mutations. Choiseul reorganized it as a distinctive second-line army. Monteynard converted its units into "provincial regiments." Saint Germain suppressed its units and made it a single recruiting pool for the regular army. Montbarrey revived it, on paper at least, so as to create more positions for officers.

The composition of cavalry regiments was changed constantly. Choiseul gave each regiment four squadrons of two companies each. Monteynard decreed three squadrons and twelve companies. Saint Germain gave each regiment five squadrons, each of which was also a company. In 1784 the number of these was reduced to four. Finally, in 1788 each regiment was composed of three squadrons of two companies each. Once again these fluctuations did not result from personal whim but from the struggle between two points of view. A few large companies were more efficient but many smaller ones provided positions for more officers.

The state of flux in which the military establishment remained was at once the cause and result of continual agitation and often violent debate among the officers of the Armée du Roi. Among the various currents and countercurrents several tendencies are clearly discernible. The first of these is a movement toward professionalism. Beginning with Belle-Isle ministers were invariably soldiers. The generalized system of military education, the peacetime maneuvers, and the "camps of instruction" are further reflections of this tendency. From the mid-eighteenth century on, officers increasingly spoke of service to "the state" or to "the nation." Does this represent an abandonment of the older, feudal concept of personal service to one's monarch and a new, more professional definition of duty? Contemporaries at least thought it did. One of them wrote: "One scarcely dares say 'serve the King'; they have substituted the expression 'serve the State.' This latter expression was in the time of Louis XIV a blasphemy. . . . The difference in expression surely denotes a difference in sentiment." [3]

A second theme, increasingly marked as the century closed, was a nationalistic one. Though many officers had been outspoken in their admiration of Frederick II, the attempts to "Prussianize" the army under Saint Germain and Puységur encountered heavy and increasing opposition. "French tactics" were devised in opposition to Prussian ones. Though the Prussian soldier might be made into an automaton, the Frenchman was still a human being. Chevalier de Ray voiced the feeling of many when he exclaimed: "Let us remain Athenians, fight the Lacedæmonians, and not imitate the Prussians." [4]

The most widespread development in military thought, and certainly the most pernicious one, was the appearance of an aristocratic reaction. In its inception, at least, it was not a contradiction to the trend toward professionalism. One of its earliest ideologues was the Chevalier d'Arc, whose *Noblesse militaire* had considerable impact after its publication in 1756. The author argued for a nobility that was a selfless and dedicated military caste, vaguely reminiscent of the Spartan timocracy. But the all too human tendency of most nobles was to see the profession of arms in terms of its benefits to them. The military spokesmen for aristocractic privilege became increasingly eloquent, perhaps through the heavy accretion of elements from the *noblesse de robe,* whose invasion of

---

3. Abbé Joseph-Alphonse de Véri, *Journal* (Paris, 1928–1932), II, 194–95.
4. *Réflexions*, p. 210.

the army Professor Ford finds "most striking." [5] The destitute provincial nobility must also have added a strident tone. It is not surprising that reform-minded ministers had the least success when their measures threatened the vested interests of the nobility. Choiseul always moved very circumspectly here. Saint Germain, by contrast, attacked sinecures, particularly those in the fashionable household troops, with a brutal directness. No diplomat, he asserted that he would rather be hated than ignored. He achieved his goal only too well. A storm of protest soon drove him from the ministry. A final experiment in reducing the hordes of useless officers was made in 1788–1789 by the Conseil de la Guerre. This body, whose guiding spirit was Guibert, represented the temporary ascendancy of the "Young Turks" of the army. Its vigorous measures produced "a wave of anger of a violence completely unexpected," which was to find its way into the *cahiers* of the second estate. [6]

The pressure which the aroused nobility brought to bear on its behalf was irresistible. Even Saint Germain was compelled to create "captains without companies" for young scions of the noble houses. Under more complacent ministers the concessions to privilege were even greater. In 1751 proof of nobility was required for admission to the newly chartered Ecole Militaire. In 1772 the same requirement was extended to the artillery schools, and in 1776 to those of the engineers. These steps are significant, for these two latter services had long been the refuge of the *roturier*. Legislation of this type culminated in the notorious ruling of 1781 that all aspirants for commissions produce four quarterings. The drive toward exclusiveness accelerated in both military and civil careers.

The army of 1789 was not what it had been in 1756. Laudable changes had been made, or at least begun. But

---

5. Franklin L. Ford, *Robe and Sword: The Regrouping of the French Aristocracy after Louis XIV* (Cambridge, Mass., 1953), p. 116.
6. Egret, *Pré-Révolution*, p. 93.

these generally involved questions of detail, and of essentially technical nature. Much that was done was subsequently undone. Fluctuations in policy created a sense of impermanence; innovations were often made at the cost of morale. The government's well-intentioned intervention in the administration of companies and regiments may have destroyed the personal bonds that had existed between officers and men and thus hastened the disintegration of the army in 1789. The spirit of the army at that critical moment was not good. The lower officers displayed an *esprit frondeur* that counted for more than a little in the early disturbances. The soldiers, inarticulate until the very eve of the Revolution, became its activists almost overnight. The Armée du Roi was one of the first victims of the Revolution. It remained for a new generation to reforge the weapon and make it the instrument of victory on a hundred battlefields.

Bibliography

Sources

[*Manuscripts*]

"Correspondance militaire" (Série A¹), MS Vols. 3470–3490, 3500–3506, 3508, 3511–3526, 3542–3546, 3548, 3550–3565, 3576–3579, 3625, 3747. "Fonds de Suède" (Série A²), MS Vols. 32–40, 43, 44, 52, 55, 56, 58–60, 62, 63, 68, 75. "Divers" (Série A⁴), Carton LXXXVII. "Mémoires historiques," MS Vol. 230. Archives de la Guerre, Vincennes.

The "Correspondance militaire" contains all of the surviving official correspondence between the court and the armies, 1757–1762. The "Fonds de Suède" are the papers of the Count of Clermont, both official and personal.

"Etat actuel des affaires générales concernant les finances du Royaume de France qui constate, 1ᵉ les revenues et dépenses du Roy, 2ᵉ les affaires extraordinaires faittes en France depuis et compris l'année 1756 jusqu'en 1763, 3ᵉ les affaires particulières qui se font annuellement dans le royaume en faveur de la Cour de Rome, des évêques, des ducs, comtes et pairs," MS 4066A. Bibliothèque de l'Arsenal, Paris.

"Etat des Finances du Royaume de France de 1755 à la fin de 1761," MS 2825. Bibliothèque Mazarine, Paris.

"Minutes d'arrêts se rapportant au département du Secrétaire d'Etat à la Guerre (1758–1760)," Série E, MS Vols. 2374, 2382, 2389. "Registre de transcriptions d'une partie des arrêts en finance (1758–1760)," Série E, MS Vols. 2680, 2681. Archives Nationales, Paris.

"Recueil des pièces relatives au séjour et à la campagne de l'armée française en Allemagne, 1757–1760," MS Vols. 639–669. Bibliothèque Municipale de Nancy, Nancy.

The official and personal papers of François-Marie Gayot, intendant of the Army of the Lower Rhine.

[*Published Documents*]

"Conseils des ministres sous Louis XV," *Revue rétrospective,* Ser. 3, III (1838), 343–72.

MATHON DE LA COUR, CHARLES-JOSEPH, ed. *Collection des comptes-rendus, pièces authentiques, états et tableaux concernant les finances de la France depuis 1758 jusqu'en 1787.* Lausanne and Paris, 1788.

Ordonnances militaires, in the library of the Archives de la Guerre, catalog no. H34.

[*Eighteenth-Century Military and Historical Works*]

BOUSSANELLE, LOUIS DE. *Observations militaires.* Paris, 1761.

CHENNEVIÈRES, FRANÇOIS DE. *Détails militaires dont la connaissance est necessaire à tous les officiers et principalement aux commissaires des guerres.* 6 vols., Paris, 1750.

COLOMBIER, JEAN. *Code de médicine militaire pour le service de terre.* 5 vols., Paris, 1772.

DUPRÉ D'AULNAY, LOUIS. *Traité général des subsistances militaires qui comprend la fourniture du pain de munition, des fourages & de la viande aux armées et aux troupes de garnisons; ensemble celle des hôpitaux & des équipages des vivres & de l'artillerie, par marché ou résultat du Conseil, à forfait ou par régie.* Paris, 1744.

GUIBERT, JACQUES-ANTOINE-HIPPOLYTE DE. *Œuvres militaires.* 5 vols., Paris, 1803.

HÉRICOURT, NICOLAS D'. *Elémens de l'art militaire.* 5 vols., Paris, 1756.

MOUFFLE D'ANGERVILLE. *Vie privée de Louis XV ou principaux événemens, particularités et anecdotes de son règne.* 4 vols., London, 1781.

SAXE, COMTE MAURICE DE. *Les rêveries, ou mémoires sur l'art de la guerre.* The Hague, 1756.

VOLTAIRE, FRANÇOIS-MARIE AROUET. *Précis du siècle de Louis XV et histoire du parlement de Paris.* Garnier Edition, Paris, 1908.

[*Memoirs, Letters, and Diaries*]

ARGENSON, RENÉ-LOUIS DE VOYER, MARQUIS D'. *Mémoires et journal.* Ed. J.-B. Rathéry. 9 vols., Paris, 1859–1867.

BARBIER, E.-J.-F. *Chronique de la régence et du règne de Louis*

XV (1718–1763); ou journal de Barbier. 8 vols., Paris, 1857.

BARENNES, JEAN. "Claude Barrière; un chirurgien périgourdin pendant la Guerre de Sept Ans. Sa correspondance de 1757 à 1764," *Revue de monde catholique,* CC (1922), 65–75.

BELLEVAL, L.-R. DE. *Souvenirs d'un chevau-léger de la garde du Roi.* Paris, 1866.

BERNIS, FRANÇOIS-JOACHIM DE PIERRES, CARDINAL DE. *Mémoires et lettres.* Ed. Frédéric Masson. 2 vols., Paris, 1878.

BESENVAL, PIERRE-VICTOR, BARON DE. *Mémoires.* Paris, 1846.

BOURCET, GÉNÉRAL PIERRE-JOSEPH DE. *Mémoires historiques sur la guerre que les Français ont soutenu en Allemagne depuis 1757 jusqu'en 1762.* 3 vols., Paris, 1792.

BROGLIE, CHARLES-FRANÇOIS, COMTE DE. *Correspondance secrète avec Louis XV.* Vol. I (1756–1766). Paris, 1956.

BROGLIE, VICTOR-FRANÇOIS, DUC DE. *Correspondance du duc de Broglie avec le prince Xavier de Saxe, comte de Lusace (1759–1761), pour servir à l'histoire de la Guerre de Sept Ans.* Ed. Duc L.-A.-V. de Broglie and H. Vernier. 4 vols., Paris, 1903.

CASTELNAU, LOUIS-JOSEPH-AMABLE DE RICHARD, BARON DE. *Lettres du baron de Castelnau, officier des carabiniers (1758–1793).* Ed. Baron de Blay de Gaix. Paris, 1911.

CHOISEUL, ETIENNE-FRANÇOIS, DUC DE. *Mémoires (1719–1785).* Ed. Fernand Calmettes. Paris, 1904.

————. *Mémoires écrits par luimême* (work of Soulavie). Paris, 1790.

CRILLON, LOUIS-ATHANASE DES BALBES DE BERTON, DUC DE. *Mémoires militaires (1731–1782).* Paris, 1791.

CROY, EMMANUEL, DUC DE. *Journal inédit.* Ed. Comte de Grouchy and Paul Cottin. Paris, 1906.

DUCLOS, CHARLES. *Mémoires secrets sur le règne de Louis XIV, la régence et le règne de Louis XV.* 2 vols., Paris, 1864.

DUFORT DE CHEVERNY, COMTE JEAN-NICOLAS. *Mémoires.* Introduction and notes by Robert de Crevecoeur. 2 vols., Paris, 1909.

DUMOURIEZ, GÉNÉRAL CHARLES-FRANÇOIS. *Galérie des aristocrates militaires et mémoires secrets.* London, 1790.

————. *Vie et mémoires du général Dumouriez.* 4 vols., Paris, 1822–1823.

FEUQUIÈRES, ANTOINE DE PAS, MARQUIS DE. *Memoirs of the late Marquis de Feuquières, Lieutenant-General of the French Army.* 2 vols., London, 1737.

FEYDEAU DE SAINT CHRISTOPHE, P. J. F. *Correspondance inédite relative à la Guerre de Sept Ans et à la Guerre de l'Indépendance Américaine.* Ed. M. Le Moy. Paris, 1921.

FREDERICK II. *Œuvres posthumes.* Decker and Voss Edition. 15 vols., Berlin, 1788.

GOETHE, JOHANN WOLFGANG. *Aus meinem Leben: Dichtung und Wahrheit* (Vol. X of *Gedenkausgabe der Werke, Briefe und Gespräche*). Zurich, 1948.

HAUSSET, MADAME NICOLLE DU. *Madame de Pompadour d'après le journal de sa femme de chambre.* Ed. Marcelle Tinayre. Paris, 1910.

HÊNAULT, PRESIDENT CHARLES-JEAN-FRANÇOIS. *Mémoires.* Ed. Marquise de Vigan. Paris, 1855.

HOEGGER, MAX. "Die Briefe des Georg Leonhard Högger von St. Gallen, Hauptmann im Schweizerregiment Waldner in französischen Diensten an seinen Vetter Burgermeister Daniel Högger in St. Gallen," *Neujahrsblatt der Feuerwerken Gesellschaft (Artillerie-Kollegium) in Zurich,* CXXXXVII (1956).

LEMOINE, JEAN, ed. *Sous Louis le Bien-Aimé. Correspondance amoureuse et militaire d'un officer pendant la Guerre de Sept Ans (1757–1765).* Paris, 1905.

LE PELLETIER, LOUIS-AUGUSTE. *Mémoires de Louis-Auguste le Pelletier, seigneur de Glatigny, lieutenant général dans les armées du roi, 1696–1769.* Paris, 1896.

LUYNES, CHARLES-PHILIPPE-ALBERT, DUC DE. *Mémoires sur la cour de Louis XV (1735–1758).* Ed. L. Dussieux and E. Soulié. 17 vols., Paris, 1860–1865.

MERCOYROL DE BEAULIEU, JACQUES. *Campagnes 1743–1763.* Ed. Marquis de Vogué and Auguste Le Sourd. Paris, 1915.

MONTALEMBERT, MARC-RENÉ, MARQUIS DE. *Correspondance de M. le marquis de Montalembert, étant employé par le roi de France à l'armée suèdoise, avec M. le marquis d'Havrincour, M. le maréchal de Richelieu, les ministres du Roi à Versailles, MM. les généraux suèdois et autres, etc., pendant les campagnes de 1757, 58, 59, 60 et 61, pour servir à l'histoire de la dernière guerre.* 3 vols., London, 1777.

MONTBAREY, ALEXANDRE-MARIE-LÉONOR DE SAINT MAURIS, PRINCE DE. *Mémoires.* 3 vols., Paris, 1826–1827.

PUISIEUX, ABBÉ. "M. de Prilly, un soldat de la Guerre de Sept Ans, d'après ses lettres," *Mémoires de la Société d'Agriculture, Commerce, Science et Arts du département de la Marne,* 1888, pp. 37–51.

RAY, CHEVALIER DE. *Réflexions et souvenirs.* Ed. Lucien Mouillard. Paris et Limoges, 1895.

RICHELIEU, MARÉCHAL LOUIS FRANÇOIS ARMAND DE PLESSIS, DUC DE. *Correspondance particulière et historique du maréchal duc de Richelieu en 1756, 1757, et 1758, avec M. Paris Duverney.* 2 vols., Paris, 1789.

————. *Mémoires authentiques du Maréchal de Richelieu (1725–1757).* Ed. A. de Boislisle. Paris, 1918.

ROCHAMBEAU, JEAN-BAPTISTE-DONATIEN DE VIMEUR, COMTE DE. *Mémoires militaires, historiques et politiques.* Ed. Luce de Lanceval. 2 vols., Paris, 1809.

SAINT GERMAIN, CLAUDE-LOUIS, COMTE DE. *Correspondance particulière du comte de Saint Germain avec M. Paris Duverney.* 2 vols., London, 1789.

————. *Mémoires.* Amsterdam, 1779.

VALFONS, CHARLES DE MATHEI, MARQUIS DE. *Souvenirs du marquis de Valfons, vicomte de Sébourg, lieutenant général des armées du Roi (1710–1786).* Ed. Marquis de Valfons and Georges Maurin. Paris, 1906.

VÉRI, ABBÉ JOSEPH-ALPHONSE DE. *Journal.* Ed. Baron Jehan de Witte. 2 vols., Paris, 1928–1932.

WIMPFFEN, LOUIS-FÉLIX, BARON DE. *Commentaires sur les mémoires du comte de Saint Germain.* London, 1780.

Authorities

[Reference Works]

Almanach royal de 1758. Paris, 1758.

Biographie universelle ancienne et moderne (Michaud). Second edition. 44 vols., Paris, 1843.

Encyclopédie, ou dictionnaire raisonné des sciences, des arts et des métiers. Ed. Denis Diderot *et al.* 17 vols., Paris, 1751–1765.

Encyclopédie méthodique (Panckoucke). *Art militaire,* 4 vols., Paris, 1784–1797. *Arts et métiers mécaniques,* 8 vols., Paris, 1782–1791.

MARION, MARCEL. *Dictionnaire des institutions de la France au XVIIIᵉ et XVIIIᵉ siècles.* Paris, 1923.

[Background Studies]

ARCHENHOLZ, JOHANN WILHELM VON. *Geschichte des siebenjährigen Krieges.* 2 vols., Berlin, n.d.

AUDOUIN, XAVIER. *Histoire de l'administration de la guerre.* 4 vols., Paris, 1811.

BABEAU, ALBERT. *La vie militaire sous l'ancien régime: Les officiers.* Paris, 1891.

————. *La vie militaire sous l'ancien régime: Les soldats.* Paris, 1891.

BACQUET, CAPITAINE D'INFANTERIE. *L'infanterie au XVIIIe siècle; l'organisation.* Paris, 1907.

BAUMANN, BERNARD VON. *Studien über die Verpflegung der Kriegsheere im Felde.* 2 vols., Leipzig and Heidelburg, 1867– 1874.

BERTHAUT, COLONEL HENRI-MARIE-AUGUSTE. *Les ingénieurs-géographes militaires, 1624–1831.* 2 vols., Paris, 1902.

BESKROVNII, L. G. *Russkaia Armiia i Flot v XVIII veke.* Moscow, 1958.

BRICE, DOCTEUR LÉON-RAOUL-MARIE AND CAPITAINE MAURICE BOTTET. *Le corps de santé militaire en France, son évolution —ses campagnes, 1708–1882.* Paris and Nancy, 1907.

BROGLIE, ALBERT, DUC DE. *Le secret du roi (1752–74).* 2 vols., Paris, 1876.

CARRÉ, HENRI. *Louis XV* (Vol. VIII, Pt. 2 of *Histoire de France illustré depuis les origines jusqu'à la Révolution,* ed. Ernest Lavisse). Paris, 1911.

————. *La noblesse de France et l'opinion publique au XVIIIe siècle.* Paris, 1920.

CARRIAS, EUGÈNE. *La pensée militaire française.* Paris, 1960.

CHASSIGNET, L.-M.-M. *Essai historique sur les institutions militaires ou la formation, l'organisation et l'administration des armées en France depuis les temps les plus reculés jusqu'en 1789.* Paris, 1869.

COLIN, COMMANDANT JEAN-LAMBERT-ALPHONSE. *Les campagnes du maréchal de Saxe.* 3 vols., Paris, 1901–1904.

————. *Les transformations de la guerre.* Paris, 1911.

CORVISIER, ANDRÉ. *L'Armée française de la fin du XVIIe siècle au ministère de Choiseul: Le soldat.* Paris, 1964.

COUSIN, J. *Le comte de Clermont et ses amis.* Paris, 1867.

CURTIS, EDWARD E. *The Organization of the British Army in the American Revolution.* New Haven, 1926.

DELBRÜCK, HANS. *Geschichte der Kriegskunst im Rahmen der politischen Geschichte.* 4 vols., Berlin, 1900–1920.

DUBLANCHY, LIEUTENANT CHARLES-NICOLAS. *Une intendance d'armée au XVIIIe siècle. Etude sur les services administratifs à l'armée de Soubise pendant la Guerre de Sept Ans, d'après la correspondance et les papiers inédits de l'intendant François-Marie Gayot.* Paris, 1908.

DURUY, ALBERT. *L'Armée royale en 1789.* Paris, 1888.

DUSSAUGE, ANDRÉ. *Etudes sur la Guerre de Sept Ans. Le ministère de Belle-Isle: Krefeld et Lütterberg (1758).* Paris, 1914.

ECKARD, WERNER, AND OTTO MORAWIETZ. *Die Handwaffen des brandenburgisch-preussisch-deutschen Heeres, 1640–1945.* Hamburg, 1957.

EGRET, JEAN. *La Pré-Révolution française (1787–1788).* Paris, 1962.

FIEFFÉ, EUGÈNE. *Histoire des troupes étrangères au service de France depuis leur origine jusqu'à nos jours et de tous les régiments levés dans les pays conquis sous la première république et l'empire.* 2 vols., Paris, 1854.

FORD, FRANKLIN L. *Robe and Sword: The Regrouping of the French Aristocracy after Louis XIV.* Cambridge, Mass., 1953.

FRAIKIN, JOSEPH. *L'industrie armurière liègeoise et le banc d'épreuves des armes à feu de Liège.* Liège, 1940.

FRÉMONT, PAUL-JEAN-MICHEL-RAOUL. *Les payeurs d'armées. Historique du service de la trésorerie et des postes aux armées, 1293–1870.* Paris, 1906.

GEBELIN, JACQUES. *Histoire des milices provinciales (1688–1791). Le tirage au sort sous l'ancien régime.* Paris, 1882.

GOOCH, G. P. *Louis XV: The Monarchy in Decline.* London, 1956.

GOTHSCHE. *Die königlichen Gewehrfabriken. Kurze Darstellung ihrer Entstehung, Entwicklung und Aufgaben.* Berlin, 1904.

GRAS, L.-J. *Historique de l'armurerie stéphanoise.* Saint Etienne, 1905.

HANTSCH, HUGO. *Die Geschichte Österreichs, 1648–1918.* Vienna, 1947.

HENNET, LÉON. *Regards en arrière. Etudes d'histoire militaire sur le XVIIIᵉ siècle. L'Etat-major.* Paris, 1911.

HICKS, JAMES E., AND ANDRÉ JANDOT. *Notes on French Ordnance, 1717–1936.* Mount Vernon, N.Y., 1938.

JÄHNS, MAX. *Geschichte der Kriegswissenschaften vornehmlich in Deutschland.* 3 vols., Munich and Leipzig, 1889–1891.

JANY, CURT. *Geschichte der Königlich-Preussischen Armee bis zum Jahre 1807.* 3 vols., Berlin, 1928–1929.

JOBEZ, ALPHONSE. *La France sous Louis XV (1715–1774).* 6 vols., Paris, 1873.

KNORR, EMIL. *Entwicklung und Gestaltung des Heeres-Sanitäts-wesens der Europäischen Staaten.* Hanover, 1880.

LAFEUILLADE, JEAN. *Les grandes lois de l'organisation. Le XVIIIe siècle. L'evolution militaire.* Paris, 1937.

LATREILLE, CAPITAINE ALBERT. *L'armée et la nation à la fin de l'ancien régime. Les derniers ministres de la guerre de la monarchie.* Paris, 1914.

LAURENCIN-CHAPELLE, PAUL. *Les archives de guerre historiques et administratives, 1688–1898.* Paris, 1898.

LÉONARD, EMILE G. *L'Armée et ses problèmes au XVIIIe siècle,* Paris, 1958.

LUÇAY, HÉLION, VICOMTE DE. *Des origines du pouvoir ministériel en France. Les secrétaires d'état depuis leur institution jusqu'à la mort de Louis XV.* Paris, 1881.

MAILATH, JOHANN. *Geschichte von Östreich.* 5 vols., Hamburg, 1850.

MANCEAU, HENRI. *La manufacture d'armes de Charleville.* Charleville, 1962.

MARGERAND, J. *Armement et équipement de l'infanterie française du XVIe au XXe siècles.* Paris, 1945.

MARION, MARCEL. *Histoire financière de la France depuis 1715.* 4 vols., Paris, 1914–1936.

MARTIN, HENRI. *Histoire de France.* Fourth edition. 17 vols., Paris, 1860.

MEIXNER, OBERSTLEUTNANT OTTO. *Historischer Rückblick auf die Verpflegung der Armeen im Felde. Lieferung I.* Vienna, 1895.

MENTION, LOUIS. *L'armée de l'ancien régime de Louis XIV à la Révolution.* Paris, n.d.

————. *Le comte de Saint Germain et ses réformes.* Paris, 1884.

MENTZEL, E. O. *Die Remontirung der preussischen Armee in ihrer historischer Entwicklung.* Berlin, 1870.

MEYER, MORITZ. *Manuel historique de la technologie des armes à feu.* Trans. A. Rieffel. 2 vols., Paris, 1838.

MICHELET, JULES. *Histoire de la Révolution Française.* 2 vols., Pléiade edition.

MOUILLARD, LUCIEN. *Les régiments sous Louis XV. Constitution de tous les corps de troupe pendant les Guerres de Succession à l'Empire et de Sept Ans.* Paris, 1882.

NOLHAC, PIERRE DE. *Madame de Pompadour et la politique d'après les documents nouveaux.* Paris, 1928.

PAJOL, GÉNÉRAL CHARLES-PIERRE-VICTOR. *Les guerres sous Louis XV.* 7 vols., Paris, 1881–1891.

PECKHAM, HOWARD. *The Colonial Wars, 1689–1762.* Chicago, 1964.

PEREY, LUCIEN. *Le duc de Nivernais.* Paris, 1891.

PERNOT, A. *Aperçu historique sur le service des transports militaires.* Paris and Limoges, 1894.

PICARD, COLONEL E., AND LIEUTENANT R. JOUAN. *L'artillerie française au XVIIIᵉ siècle.* Paris, 1906.

PIERQUIN, H. *La juridiction du point d'honneur et le tribunal des maréchaux sous l'ancien régime.* Paris, 1904.

REBOUL, COLONEL FRÉDÉRIC. *La vie au dix-huitième siècle. L'armée.* Paris, 1931.

RIBAUCOURT, E. DE. *La vie et les exploits de J.-C. Fischer, brigadier des armées du Roy Louis XV, fondateur et commandant le corps des chasseurs (1743–1761), chef du service des renseignements.* Paris, 1929.

ROUSSET, CAMILLE. *Le comte de Gisors, 1732–1758.* Paris, 1868.

————. *Histoire de Louvois et de son administration politique et militaire.* 4 vols., Paris, 1864.

SARS, COMTE R. DE. *Le recrutement de l'armée permanente sous l'ancien régime.* Paris, 1920.

SAUTAI, MAURICE, AND EDMOND DESBRIÈRE. *La cavalerie de 1740 à 1789.* Paris, 1904.

THOUMAS, GÉNÉRAL CHARLES-ANTOINE. *Les transformations de l'armée française. Essais d'histoire et de critique sur l'état militaire en France.* 2 vols., Paris, 1887.

TUETEY, LOUIS. *Les officiers sous l'ancien régime, nobles et roturiers.* Paris, 1908.

WADDINGTON, RICHARD. *La Guerre de Sept Ans.* 5 vols., Paris, 1894–1907.

WESTPHALEN, CHRISTIAN HEINRICH PHILLIP EDLER VON. *Geschichte der Feldzüge des Herzogs Ferdinand von Braunschweig-Lüneburg.* 6 vols., Berlin, 1859–1872.

WHITWORTH, REX. *Field Marshal Lord Ligonier: A Story of the British Army, 1702–1770.* Oxford, 1958.

[*Articles*]

ANON. "Le commissariat des guerres, son organisation, son évolution, ses attributions," *Revue de l'intendance militaire,* XLVI (1958), 40–78.

————. "Equipage de Louis-François-César de Bouet, mestre

de camp, chevalier de Saint Louis, chef de la 3ᵉ brigade de carabiniers," *Carnet de la sabretache,* X (1902), 417–420.

——————. "Le service des poudres," *Revue historique de l'armée,* XIX, No. 2 (1964), 85–108.

——————. "Une affiche de recruteurs, 1757," *Carnet de la sabretache,* XI (1903), 380–383.

ANTOINE, MICHAEL. "Les conseils de finances sous le règne de Louis XV," *Revue d'histoire moderne et contemporaine,* V (1958), 161–200.

BADER, CLARISSE. "Un éducateur de l'armée française: le général de Melfort," *Revue des questions historiques,* New Series, XXIII (January, 1900), 148–187.

BESKROVNII, L. G. "Proizvodstvo Voruzheniia i Boepripasov na russkikh Zavodakh v pervoi Polovine XVIII v.," *Istoricheskie Zapiski.,* No. 36 (1951), 101–141.

COQUELLE, P. "Occupation de Hanovre par les français pendant la Guerre de Sept Ans," *Revue des études historiques,* LXII (1896), 62–73.

CORVISIER, ANDRÉ. "Un problème social de l'ancien régime: la composition de l'armée," *Actualité historique,* No. 22 (1958), 3–9.

DERUELLE, G. "Aperçu historique sur les fabrications d'armement en France," *Revue historique de l'Armée,* XII, No. 4 (1956), 89–101.

DES CILLEULS, JEAN. "Les aumôniers aux armées de l'ancien régime," *Revue historique de l'armée,* XII, No. 3 (1956), 5–16.

——————. "Le service de santé à l'intérieur sous l'ancien régime," *Revue historique de l'armée,* XI, No. 3 (1955), 57–74.

——————. "L'organisation du service de santé aux armées de l'ancien régime," *Revue historique de l'armée,* IX, No. 2 (1953), 7–36.

DUSSAUGE, ANDRÉ. "Le ministère de Belle-Isle. La crise du recrutement," *Revue d'histoire,* L (1913), 414–453.

——————. "Le ministère de Belle-Isle. Les reformes de 1758," *Revue d'histoire,* XLV (1912), 353–377; XLVI (1912), 1–28.

ELIE, HUBERT. "Le marquis de Courteille, ambassadeur de Louis XV en Suisse et le recrutement des troupes suisses au service de la France," *Revue historique de l'armée,* X, No. 4 (1956), 5–22.

GAUDIN, M. "Historique de la fabrication des armes lègères," *Revue historique de l'armée*, XII, No. 4 (1956), 115–126.

HERLAUT, CAPITAINE AUGUSTE-PHILIPPE. "Les abus du recrutement au XVIIIe siècle," *Revue du XVIIIe siècle*, I, No. 3 (July-September, 1913), 294–301.

LOBIT, JEAN. "Prévôts généraux de la marechaussée," *Bulletin de la société bordelaise*, LXXXII, No. 291 (1958), 295–308.

MAHON, CAPITAINE PATRICE. "Un commissaire des guerres sous l'ancien regime. Pierre-Nicolas de Lasalle (père du Général Lasalle)," *Carnet de la sabretache*, VIII (1900), 343–353.

MILLOT, A. "Le fusil à manivelle, 1758," *Carnet de la sabretache*, III (1895), 233–240.

————. "La table des officiers généraux dans la Guerre de Sept Ans: 1758," *Carnet de la sabretache*, II (1894), 417–432.

MOLIAS, D., et al. "Le corps de l'intendance militaire," *Revue historique de l'armée*, XIII, No. 4 (1957), 83–124.

MONTBAS, VICOMTE DE. "Choiseul et la résurrection de l'armée de Rossbach," *Revue des transactions de l'académie des sciences morales et politiques*, année 107 (1954), pp. 48–62.

MOSES, COLONEL ROBERT S. "Of Plagues and Pennants," *Military Review*, XLV, No. 5 (May, 1965), 71–84.

TITEUX, EUGÈNE. "Le chevalier le Pelletier, lieutenant-général des armées du Roi (1697–1765)," *Carnet de la sabretache*, VIII (1900), 732–738.

Index